Susannah Hayward was born in London, grew up on England's south coast and hot-footed it straight back to the big smoke as soon as she was old enough to leave school. Armed with nothing more than a couple of shorthand and typing certificates, a reasonable command of the English language and the gift of the gab, she supported herself by doing a variety of low-grade, low-paid jobs before stumbling joyfully into journalism via the advertising department of a rock music paper.

In the early 1980s, Susannah completed a course in journalism at the London College of Printing and since then, has worked as a news and feature writer, a sub-editor, production editor and chief sub-editor on a wide variety of mainstream publications including – in the UK – *Honey*, *Woman*, *Woman's Realm*, *Living* and *Elle*; and – in Australia – *Woman's Day*, *Family Circle*, *New Woman*, *Good Weekend*, *Mother & Baby*, *She*, *New Weekly* and *The Bulletin*. She has also edited two non-fiction books. Susannah migrated to Australia in 1988 and currently lives in Sydney.

SUSANNAH HAYWARD

Breathe easy

the friendly

stop-smoking guide

for women

PENGUIN BOOKS

Penguin Books Australia Ltd
487 Maroondah Highway, PO Box 257
Ringwood, Victoria 3134, Australia
Penguin Books Ltd
Harmondsworth, Middlesex, England
Penguin Putnam Inc.
375 Hudson Street, New York, New York 10014, USA
Penguin Books Canada Limited
10 Alcorn Avenue, Toronto, Ontario, Canada M4V 3B2
Penguin Books (NZ) Ltd
Cnr Rosedale and Airborne Roads, Albany, Auckland, New Zealand
Penguin Books (South Africa) (Pty) Ltd
5 Watkins Street, Denver Ext 4, 2094, South Africa
Penguin Books India (P) Ltd
11, Community Centre, Panchsheel Park, New Delhi 110 017, India

First published by Penguin Books Australia Ltd 2000

3 5 7 9 10 8 6 4 2

Cover and text design by Erika Budiman, Penguin Design Studio
Typeset in 9.75/14 pt Sabon by Post Pre-press Group, Brisbane, Queensland
Printed and bound in Australia by Australian Print Group, Maryborough, Victoria

National Library of Australia
Cataloguing-in-Publication data:

Hayward, Susannah.
Breathe easy: the friendly stop-smoking guide for women.

Includes index.

ISBN 0 14 028824 4.

1. Smoking – Prevention. 2. Women – Tobacco use. I. Title.
II. Title: Friendly stop-smoking guide for women.

362.296082

www.penguin.com.au

Dedicated to Dorothy, Ben, Jenny and Nan

Contents

Acknowledgements

AT THE RISK OF sounding like an Oscar winner, I'd
like to offer my heartfelt thanks, first and foremost, to
all the women who took part in my survey; to Beverley
Malzard for her friendship, moral support and dogged
distribution of my questionnaires; to Patricia Waters,
Christine Shepherd, Dr Linda Mann and Professor Neil
Grunberg for giving their professional advice so gener-
ously; to Dr Bobbie Jacobson for permission to use
material from her books; to Sarah Walker, Robin Barker
and Diana Simmonds for their inspiration and for allowing me to pick their brains; to Clare Grundy, Mike
Eastland, Judy Boydell, Denise Shaw and Rosemary
Pryor for their friendship, for listening, and for believing
in me; to Trish Lake for knocking on the right doors; to
Lisa Mills for answering; and to Fiona Daniels for her
professionalism, enthusiasm and diplomacy.

Foreword by Penny Cook

I THINK I KNEW I had a problem with smoking when I found myself looking through the ashtray for a butt that had at least enough length to get a couple of puffs. Actually, I think I knew I had a problem twenty years earlier when I started smoking because a friend of mine smoked and I thought he was the ant's pants. He now tells me I said I smoked so that I wouldn't gain weight (it didn't work).

I have what you might call an addictive personality. Cigarettes, alcohol, chocolate, chocolate mousse, in fact anything sweet, and coffee. Over the years I have occasionally been able to stop taking one, but never all at once. When I stopped drinking coffee, I seemed to increase my smoking and nearly overdosed on chamomile tea. When I stopped drinking alcohol, I seemed to increase my smoking and nearly overdosed on caffeine-free Diet Coke. When I stopped eating chocolate I seemed to increase my smoking and nearly overdosed on chips (potato, soya, corn, prawn, and hot and greasy). When I stopped smoking cigarettes I seemed to overdose on coffee, chamomile tea, champagne, chocolates, anything sweet, chips, and Vitamin C tablets (someone said that would help get over the addiction). I have given up smoking many times – I am an expert.

This bout of not-smoking time will have been four years on 19 February 2000. However, I know that I am still a smoker type. I need to constantly remember to be wary.

I think Susannah Hayward is terrific for putting into words so many of the steps to breathing easily and so many of the pitfalls. If *Breathe Easy* can help even one person get off and stay off then she is onto a winner. I wish this book had been around for my struggle, but I'm glad it's here now.

Penny Cook is an actress and a reformed smoker. She has smoked through many jobs in the film, television and theatre industry in Australia over the last twenty years. She now tries NOT to smoke.

It is now proved beyond

doubt that smoking is one

of the leading causes

of statistics.

Fletcher Knebel, quoted
in Reader's Digest,
December 1961

Introduction

NICOTINE IS AT LAST being acknowledged as a drug that hooks users in much the same way as heroin. It is, in fact, one of the most addictive drugs known to humankind. While not everyone who smokes cigarettes will become addicted – just as not every person who uses heroin will fit the stereotypical image of the strung-out junkie – it is the addiction to nicotine that keeps us smoking when our good sense tells us we shouldn't.

Yet despite the overwhelming evidence that nicotine is powerfully addictive, popular belief still has it that cigarette smoking is a 'habit' indulged in by people whose sole purpose in life is to annoy the hell out of non-smokers and frustrate the medical profession; or that those of us who continue to smoke, in spite of the dangers, do so because we are too stupid to believe that any one of those horrible diseases could happen to us.

If you are a smoker reading this, you know that's not true. You are not stupid, even though as a smoker you often *feel* stupid. You are well aware of the dangers of smoking and you desperately want to stop, as most smokers do. You have probably made a couple of attempts to stop in the past and found the withdrawal symptoms just too hard to handle. Or you may have given up several times in the past with varying degrees of success. Some of you might even have been able to stop for a year or two, but you just can't seem to get free of the weed for good.

So what's wrong with you? Nothing. Put simply, for many women the quit campaigns don't work. And the reason they don't work is because they are not designed for women. While not deliberately aimed at men they are based on the principle that what will work for men will work for women. It won't. Because men and women are different. If you think I'm stating the bleedin' obvious, oblivious is how I would describe those responsible for the quit campaigns.

Despite plenty of scientific evidence that women respond differently to all kinds of drugs, including nicotine, the quit campaigns and programs do not reflect this. Neither do they reflect the fact that women and men smoke differently – for different reasons and under different circumstances. They also fail to take into account that when women stop smoking we experience a whole host of withdrawal symptoms that men mostly do not, including an often dramatic and unwanted weight gain. Then there are a host of other side-effects which make quitting smoking while trying to live a normal, everyday life extremely difficult. Which perhaps explains why women and girls are not only failing to respond to the current quit strategies but are actually smoking more or less as much now as when it was socially acceptable! In fact, for a time in the 1990s, with the anti-smoking campaign on 'High' and the messages at their most gruesome, smoking rates for women actually increased.

No one need take my word for it. According to the Australian Institute of Health & Welfare (AIHW) in its 1998 Household Survey, around 4 000 000 Australians are currently still puffing away – some 28.9 per cent of men and 23.9 per cent of women. Yet a 1995 survey by the government's own Australian Bureau of Statistics (ABS) puts the rate of female smokers at 20.3 per cent. At the same time, the ABS survey notes glumly that 'the proportion [of people] taking up smoking has declined only slightly since the late 1970s'. So much for two decades of vigorous anti-smoking campaigning! Meanwhile, back in the mid-1940s, when smoking was still socially acceptable, 72 per cent of Australian males lit up compared with only 26 per cent of women. So while time and the tyranny of the anti-smoking lobby have seen smoking rates among men plummet, the rates for women have hardly changed at all.

More worrying is the AIHW survey's conclusion that 'generally, the quantities of cigarettes smoked by female smokers exceeds those of male smokers'. And it isn't just the die-hards who are still lighting up. Some 400 000, or one in ten, smokers are teenagers between the ages of 14 and 19, with girls outnumbering the boys by around 10 000. Overseas, a 1998 study by Britain's Cancer

Research Campaign found that teenage girls are taking up smoking in their droves specifically to lose weight. Meanwhile, the Australian Medical Association (AMA) claims that currently between one in three and one in four pregnant women smokes.

So, what about those quit campaigns? The warnings on the cigarette packs: Your Smoking Harms Others; Smoking Kills; Smoking Will Harm Your Baby. Or those stomach-churning TV commercials showing arteries clogged by something resembling congealed rice pudding; or the one that shows a blood clot purportedly from the brain of a young person who suffered a stroke through smoking. Or the newspaper headlines proclaiming 'Smoking Mums Kill Their Babies'. These cruel and often crude anti-tobacco messages make us feel guilty, anxious, angry, resentful, frightened, discriminated against and under siege. In other words, they create the kind of feelings that cause us to light up in the first place! For women, these campaigns are so flawed that instead of questioning why so many are still smoking, we should be marvelling that so many of us have managed to stop.

I gave up smoking just over two years ago after being a die-hard (no pun intended) puffer for 27 years. It was one of the best – and most difficult – things I've ever done. To be free of this pernicious addiction sent my confidence soaring and convinced me there was nothing I couldn't achieve if I set my mind to it . . . including writing the book that didn't exist when I was going through seven shades of hell – much of it unnecessary – trying to stop smoking.

I did it the hard way because I was missing some vital information and support that could have made a difference. That information and support is all here in this book. And although I would be insulting your intelligence if I said my book will make giving up smoking easy, with the facts at your fingertips you will find it easier than I did, and easier than you found it the last time you tried to stop.

My approach to this problem is neither academic nor scientific. I would not be qualified to write from such a lofty position since I have no academic or scientific training. So combining my non-scientific qualifications – being once a chronically addicted smoker, with 18 years' experience as a researcher and journalist – I have come up with what I believe is an honest, empathetic and achievable guide to stopping smoking *and* staying stopped. In the process, I reckon I have read every quit-smoking book/booklet/leaflet/newspaper and magazine article that's ever been written. I read most of them over the years I was failing miserably to give up and I read them all again – plus a few more besides – with the benefit of hindsight while I was researching this book.

But more importantly, I've talked with and listened to the *true* experts on giving up smoking. The women who smoke and who wish they didn't. Those who have tried to stop and been unsuccessful. And the women who have stopped and who are justifiably proud, but who know the process would have been a whole lot easier with a little more help and empathy.

In order to reach them, I compiled two detailed questionnaires – one for smokers and one for ex-smokers. Then, using the power of advertising combined with my powers of persuasion over family, friends, colleagues, casual acquaintances and their family, friends, colleagues and casual acquaintances, I sent the questionnaires out to over 400 women from three different countries. Women of all ages, all walks of life, all with varying degrees of nicotine addiction. In this book you'll meet some of these women and hear their stories. They are women like you and women like me.

The ex-smokers you'll meet in this book are all recent quitters. At the time of writing some had been smoke free for a matter of weeks or a few months, while most – myself included – had been ex-smokers for two years or less, so our recall of the highs and lows of weed elimination is strong and reliable. This is important because the passing of time can play tricks on the memory. You've only got to look at childbirth to see how that works. You don't exactly forget the pain, but as time goes by it gets downgraded in your mind to the point where you think it wasn't so bad after all. This can happen with giving up smoking too.

In fact, stopping smoking is a bit like having a baby, only in some ways it's better. When the proverbial watermelon has finally passed through an orifice designed to accommodate nothing larger than a plum, you feel deep joy, wonder, relief and a terrific sense of achievement – but when you give up smoking there's the added bonus of bright, clear skin, fresh breath, increased energy, improved health and all those extra dollars in your pocket. What are you waiting for?

From the start of this project I've been asked why my book is aimed only at women. I believe I go some of the way towards answering that question at the beginning of this introduction, but the answer is also that I have first-hand knowledge of being a woman and of giving up smoking. If you accept that gender makes a difference here, then it's clear I don't have the right credentials to speak on men's behalf. But more importantly they don't need me to. I aimed my book solely at women smokers because I believe the definitive stop-smoking guide for men has already been written – by an inspirational *male* ex-smoker, whose book details I'm happy to share upon request.

If you are buying my book as a gift for someone dear to you as an incentive for her to give up smoking, don't forget to stick around to offer some ongoing support when she takes the plunge. And if you are a smoker on the verge of breaking the hold that nicotine has had on your life so far, I say go forward with confidence. You can do it. You know you can. And soon, much sooner than you think, you are going to feel as I did: proud, excited, back in control of your life, and ready to tackle the next ambition on your wish list!

Susannah Hayward, Sydney, 2000

To err is human

but it feels divine.

M A E   W E S T

Confessions of a reformed smoker

'IF SHE CAN DO IT, anyone can.' This wry observa-
tion was made by a friend after I had been free of the
weed for around six months. She was right to be
impressed. I was pretty impressed myself. At the time
she made the comment I was 40 years old and until that
momentous day six months before, I had smoked cigarettes every single day for 27 years.

I grew up in a smoking household, and graduated
from having the odd sneaky puff here and there from
about the age of 11 to smoking my first whole cigarette
at the age of 13. Of course, I immediately threw up, but
that was okay – just a normal teenage rite of passage
and it didn't put me off at all. I persevered and apart
from two dismal and very brief (one lasted just five
days!) attempts to stop that were made more than ten
years apart, I had smoked my way through my entire
teenage years plus another 20 years.

I was a truly dedicated smoker. I smoked when
I was happy and when I was sad, when I was tense
and when I was relaxed, when I was celebrating and

commiserating, in sickness and in health, in love and in labour. For at least 18 years, I smoked a pack a day and sometimes two. My smoking day used to begin before my eyes were properly open in the morning and end when they could barely stay open at night. Everywhere I went my cigarettes came too. I smoked at work in the days when you could. I smoked in the theatre and the cinema, on public transport, and even in hospitals, in the days when you could. I smoked in the street. I smoked in every room in my house – and in every room in everybody else's house. I smoked in bed and in the bath. I could clean the house and smoke, cut the grass and smoke, brush my teeth and smoke, and even pee and smoke, although I drew the line at number twos!

And at two a.m. on a Saturday night, when the lights were low, the ashtrays were full, the cigarette packets were empty – and I was nowhere near ready to call it a night – I would turn into the bitch junkie from hell. If I couldn't bully whomever I was with into trawling the streets in search of an all-night petrol station, I'd plunge my hand into the overflowing ashtrays, pull out the dogends, dismantle the longest ones and, using rolly papers, re-roll the mound of tobacco into something (barely) smokable.

I know. I know. It's utterly disgusting, but that's the desperation of a drug addict for you. If you're a young person reading this, I hope it puts you off smoking for life. As for the rest of you, go on, admit it – you've done it too. And even if you haven't sunk that low, I bet there's been at least one occasion when a late-night craving has led you to pick your way through the ashtrays in search of a butt that's long enough to straighten out and re-smoke.

Over the years I've known many smokers, and even my fellow heavies could manage a day or two's break from smoking on special occasions – like when they were sick or hospitalised, for instance. Not me. For 27 years, I smoked through all the usual ailments, like sore throats, colds, full-blown flu, bronchitis, a bad bout of glandular fever (is there a good bout of glandular fever?) and two lots of minor surgery.

I can hardly believe it now, but even on the actual days of surgery – both with general anaesthetic – my smoking career hardly missed a beat. The first operation, for the removal of two wisdom teeth, took place in London in the 1970s, in the days when smoking was still permitted on the wards. I remember coming round from the anaesthetic and, with my mouth full of blood, stitches and cotton wadding, and still barely conscious, reaching for my cigarettes. A friendly nurse helped me get one out of the packet and light it.

My second medical incarceration was also in London, in a brand new teaching hospital which, in 1981, allowed no smoking on its gleaming wards. Again, immediately after surgery and as sore as hell, I came round in a deserted eight-bed gynaecological ward badly needing a cigarette. I dragged myself out of bed and staggered down the hall where I found the ward's other walking wounded puffing away in the TV lounge (together with most of the nursing shift, I might add).

I spent most of my two-day hospital stay in that smelly, smoky room gossiping, revealing and being revealed to, and laughing until I hurt (even more).

I'm convinced that the banning of smoking on women's gynaecological wards in the democratic world in the 1980s was probably the start of a camaraderie between smokers that remains to this day. Some of the warmest, funniest, most tolerant women I have ever met have been total strangers forced together by a mutual need for nicotine. And I know plenty of warm, funny, tolerant women who have never smoked a cigarette in their lives. And, I'm sad to say, some of the most humourless, intolerant bitches I have ever met have been reformed smokers.

In your quest to stop smoking there will be moments when your sense of humour falters and sometimes even deserts you. Mine was often stretched to the limit during my first three months as an ex-smoker. My partner has the scars (metaphorically speaking) to prove it. But the biggest challenge came around the time of my friend's 'If she can do it, anyone can' comment. Because what my friend was too polite to say was that I'd lost an addiction . . . and gained one humdinger of a weight problem.

At first, I'd been so intent on getting free of the weed that I'd barely noticed the weight piling on. And after six months of not smoking, I was well past the stage of getting that 'empty feeling' that causes many ex-smokers to head for the fridge or the sweet jar. Yet my clothes just kept getting tighter and tighter so that by the time I'd been an ex-smoker for one year, I had gone up from a size 8 to a 14. I was heavier than I'd ever been in my life, including when I was pregnant, and on my 149-centimetre (4 feet 11 inches) frame this extra flesh did not look good. And although I was neither as vain nor as insecure about my appearance as I had been in my 20s, my self-esteem took a nosedive.

I carried all this blubber – and my unhappiness – around with me until I began researching this book. That's when I discovered a perfectly logical and scientific reason for the weight gain. That it had nothing to do with me being greedy or weak-willed, or needing oral gratification, or my relationship with food/my mother, or being an addictive personality, or any other psychological reason. What I discovered was that this weight gain is physiological. Put simply, when you remove your body's nicotine supply, it goes loopy.

Of course, life would have been easier if I'd known all this *before* I smoked my last cigarette. But I suppose enlightenment came better late than never. Once I understood what had been going on all those months, I managed to lose all the weight I wanted. But I did it the hard way. You won't have to. Later in the book, I explain exactly what happens to your body when you stop smoking, and how you can avoid putting on that weight in the first place. Once you know that, you have the single most annoying and long-lasting withdrawal symptom of giving up smoking licked in advance. But if you are one of the many ex-smokers still battling the bulge, Chapter 16 is just for you.

Remember, no one can make you feel inferior without your consent.

Eleanor Roosevelt

2

Why this drug is such a drag

'SOMEONE IS FINALLY Telling the Truth!' screamed
a 1997 Sydney newspaper headline in a typeface so big
it should at least have been announcing the outbreak of
a major war. But no, it was merely informing us that the
head of one of America's big five tobacco companies
had publicly confessed that smoking is bad for you.
According to the article this frank admission had only
taken them 33 years . . . which was when the US
Surgeon General first told the world that smoking
causes lung cancer and other serious diseases.

That story got me thinking about my misbegotten
youth and my old headmistress, a stern-faced, white-
haired career 'Miss', who ruled her provincial English
girls' school with great pride and the proverbial rod of
iron. A rabid anti-smoker, this formidable woman must
have known all about that 1964 Surgeon General's
report because in the late 1960s, some years before the
first government health warnings appeared anywhere in
the world, she was regularly lecturing her girls, in particular those of us who habitually got caught smoking

in the toilets, that cigarettes were addictive, caused lung cancer and anyway, she said, were an absolute waste of money.

Although my headmistress didn't have the benefit of today's technology to reinforce her message, colour transparencies of a dead smoker's lungs projected onto a three-metre-wide screen were very effective. 'Yuk, I'm never smoking again,' we'd all say sincerely . . . for as long as it took us to conclude, with typical schoolgirl logic, that the owner of those horribly diseased lungs was probably absolutely ancient – 40, at least – so must have died of old age rather than smoking. Then we'd breathe a deep sigh of relief (deep breathing is still possible for teenage smokers) and head straight for the toilets, film show and lecture forgotten.

Like me, the majority of women set themselves on the road to nicotine addiction during their teenage years, with the ages of 13 to 18 being the most common. Just a few of those who responded to my survey admitted to taking their first puff between the ages of 9 and 12. Fewer still took it up after those impressionable childhood/teenage years, and all of these women gave a traumatic experience – either a relationship break-up or the death of someone close to them – as the reason.

The death of my best friend triggered my smoking. I got through all the adolescent peer-group pressure at school without smoking, but at my friend's death I thought my life was over. Picking up a cigarette was

a conscious decision to put the lid on my feelings.
Angel, 34, a smoker for 15 years, smokes up to 50 a day.

The overwhelming majority of my smokers – 98 per cent – cited peer-group pressure as the number one reason for lighting up that first cigarette. Other reasons given were to rebel, to help ease the pain of an unhappy childhood and to appear cool and sophisticated. No surprises there, but what did surprise me was that all these reasons for taking up smoking were given by women of all ages, including the twentysomethings who have grown up with those increasingly gruesome health warnings in their faces. Gee, those campaigns are working a treat, aren't they?

Seeing movie stars, supermodels and other popular public figures puffing away unquestionably reinforces the idea that smoking is cool and sophisticated. This is what the experts believe and some 44 per cent of my respondents agreed. I actually find this a bit of a thorny issue. To expect health professionals, politicians and others who set themselves up as arbiters of acceptable behaviour to practise what they preach is one thing. But the concept of imposing the title 'role model' on some individual who is simply trying to earn a living by acting, singing or advertising expensive clothes, and holding them accountable for the behaviour of their peers, makes me feel profoundly uncomfortable. Most of us make one or two choices in this life that we later regret. But whatever we might tell ourselves in moments of self-pity, ultimately they were *our* choices. I don't see how shifting the responsibility for those bad choices onto others helps us. It certainly doesn't help us to avoid making similar mistakes in the future.

Of course, those who take the moral high ground believe our public figures, however youthful, should 'set an example', but I think that's a big ask.

Interestingly, the anti-smoking lobby's biggest baddie, cigarette advertising, came nowhere on the list of smoking influences for my respondents. Just six per cent thought those glossy images that were once so familiar on billboards, in the media, at the movies and trackside at sporting events had affected their smoking habits. I agree. Like most movie-goers, I loved those quirky Benson & Hedges cinema ads of the 1980s. As well as being stylish and clever, they were better produced than some of the movies we'd gone to see, but they didn't make me switch brands.

high anxiety

There's no doubt about it, a smoker's lot these days is not a happy one. Where once we enjoyed the freedom to light up as and when we pleased, and non-smokers had to like it or lump it, these days the only place you can really relax with a cigarette is in the privacy of your own home. Or can you? If you've got children in the house or an anti-smoking partner, the term 'relax' is a bit of a misnomer. There's nothing remotely relaxing

about feeling the full weight of a loved one's disap-
proval every time you light up. Or being banished to the
backyard to smoke, come rain or shine. Or opening up
your cigarette packet and finding messages like
'Mummy, if you get lung cancer and die, I'll be an
orphan' tucked inside, written in poignantly childish
handwriting.

That last little gem was the handiwork of a friend's
12-year-old daughter. It was just one of a repertoire of
crude but creative guilt trips for kids to lay on parents,
supplied by another rabidly anti-smoking teacher. As well
as the notes, they included hiding packs of cigarettes
around the house and standing back smirking while
Mum tears the place apart trying to find them; putting
pinprick holes in individual cigarettes making it impossi-
ble to inhale the damned things properly; and daughter
coughing and spluttering like a TB sufferer every time
Mum and Dad light up. Did it work? What do you
think?

> **I spend my evenings on the back step smoking my
> head off to isolate myself from my two teenage
> daughters and have time out. In winter, I freeze my
> butt off. When stressed I chain smoke and when pre-
> menstrual, they don't want to know me anyway.**
> *Sandi, 45, a smoker for 31 years, smokes 20–25 a day.*

But being nagged, thwarted and banished from the
house by your holier-than-thou offspring is the least of

a smoker's worries these days. If you can dispense with the guilt, you can always pull rank on the opinionated little monsters by reminding them who pays the bills. It's when you step outside the front door that the harsh reality of life as a smoker really hits you. Since introducing health warnings on cigarette packets in 1973, Australia has pursued the anti-smoking message with great gusto. We now have some of the toughest restrictions in the world and the despotic anti-smoking lobby is still not satisfied. At the time of writing, they had their sights set on the few remaining public places in which smokers can still light up – i.e. bars, restaurants (in which South Australia implemented a total smoking ban in January 1999) and outdoor areas such as parks, beaches and sporting stadia. One Sydney council even proposed to ban its outworkers from smoking in their own homes on the grounds that the said homes are 'a designated workplace'.

Of course, it's all very admirable from the point of view of the nation's health. It's just a crying shame that what began as a worthwhile campaign to educate the population on the perils of smoking has turned into an all-out war against people who smoke. And let's not forget that via tobacco tax, the hapless smoker is paying dearly for this government-approved campaign of harassment and discrimination. The Feds currently pocket between 65 and 70 per cent of the recommended retail price of each pack of cigarettes; that's approximately $4.90 for your average pack of 25, which all adds up to a nice little earner of around $4.6 billion per annum.

a day in the life of a smoker

Let's look at what the poor smoker has to put up with these days. After a night's sleep of around six to eight hours your nicotine levels are reduced to nothing. So in the morning, an addicted smoker will have some topping up to do. The World Health Organisation (WHO) defines an addicted smoker as someone who smokes their first cigarette of the day soon after waking, their second some 30 minutes later, and their third within the hour. They could have been talking about me, or three-quarters of the smokers who answered my survey – or about you.

> **I have my first while I'm waiting for the kettle to boil after staggering out of bed. I have my second while drinking my short black and surveying the day – about 10 minutes later – and I can usually squeeze in another in between my shower, making lunches etc., about 30 minutes after that.** *Sandi, 45, a smoker for 31 years, smokes 20–25 a day.*

You are now ready to face the day. If you drive to work you can puff away to your heart's content for as long as your journey lasts. *At the moment.* Because you can bet your life someone is looking at ways to stop you doing

that, especially if you have children in the car. If you're
at the mercy of public transport, you'll just have to light
up on the way to catching your non-smoking bus, train,
ferry, taxi, plane. Then you can puff away again when
you get off at the other end, until you arrive at work. I
don't know about you, but in all my 27 years as a
smoker I never perfected the art of keeping a cigarette
dry in the rain, or lighting one up in a stiff wind. And I
never stopped feeling like an idiot for trying.

Whatever form of transport you use to get to work,
and however you earn a crust when you get there, the
chances are you'll be doing it in a smoke-free environment. Eighty-six per cent of my smokers told me theirs
was a non-smoking workplace (the remainder were
either self-employed or not in the workforce).

the evolution of the smoko

But then there's the smoko. It's deeply entrenched in the
Australian culture. For now, anyway. Since the staff
canteen (if you have one) and other rest areas (if you
have any) are likely to be non-smoking, for most of you
this will usually involve heading for your workplace's
nearest exit and standing around outside, often in full
view of pitying or contemptuous passers-by, who look
even more contemptuous when you ash and stub out on
the ground because there's nowhere else to put it.

Stressful though the smoko is, enjoy it while you
can because the Time and Motion branch of the

omnipresent anti-smoking lobby are onto you. You can't see them but they've got you covered the minute you leave your work station. Stopwatches and calculators in hand, they time your smoke break, add it to that of everybody else they've been spying on that day and miraculously come up with the number of working hours you are costing Business and Your Country. Then they think of an impressive dollar figure and quadruple it, issue a media release and hey presto, another anti-smoker headline is born: 'Smokers Cost Billions in Lost Productivity'.

It was only in my last seven years as a smoker that I couldn't smoke at work. And how easy or difficult I found this depended on two things: whether the work was stimulating and whether or not I was feeling valued and respected. Achieving both at the same time was a tall order. Several times I managed one without the other. Not perfect but quite bearable. But on the occasions when I felt neither stimulated nor valued, not being able to smoke at work was a problem for me. Then I would nip out a couple of times a day and join the other social pariahs on the pavement.

I apologise to past employers for any lost productivity this may have caused. But bosses whose staff are taking more than the usual number of smokos might try looking within their work environment for some answers. It will come as no surprise to anyone to discover that stress is a major trigger for women to smoke. When I asked my smokers what makes them want to

smoke more than usual, 83 per cent cited work press-
ures as a reason. And when I asked my ex-smokers if
they still get the urge to smoke, and if so in what circumstances, 64 per cent cited pressure at work.

And what of headlines such as 'Smokers Take More
Sickies'? Like 'Smokers Cost Billions in Lost
Productivity', that one infuriates me, because as well as
it being hostile, inflammatory and discriminatory, I
think it's a bit cheeky accusing people who collectively
contribute $4.6 billion a year in tobacco tax alone – in
addition to income tax and the rest – of cheating the
community. Anyway, we all know that headline should
read 'Over-worked, Under-valued and Poorly Managed
Workers Take More Sickies'. But when the media takes
a questionable piece of research and publishes it without question, it means no one cares whether it's true or
not. Meanwhile, at job interviews these days employers
are quite legally asking 'Do you smoke?' . . .

time to play

Your working day is over and you have a night out with
a few colleagues. You start at the pub, which is one of
the few places a smoker can still sit down and smoke in
peace – for the time being anyway. The smoke-free bar
became a reality for Californian drinkers on 1 January
1998. Despite talk of some 1960s-style resistance by
unhappy smokers, at the time of writing this law still
stands and is coming to a bar near you. And whatever

you might think of the asthmatic who deliberately spent an evening in a smoky night club then went rushing off to a lawyer screaming about passive smoking, the fact is, she won. The writing's not only on the wall . . . it's all over the statute books.

After the pub you fancy taking in a movie or a play or a concert. You can have a few smokes on the pavement before you go in because you can't smoke inside, not even in the bars. Never mind – the movie/play/concert was great, even if you did get a bit distracted towards the end when the nicotine urge became too strong. Those long movies, especially, are a killer.

Time for a bite to eat. Your favourite restaurant has smoking and non-smoking sections. What a shame you didn't book as smoking is full tonight. Never mind, the place down the road's good and the owner reckons hell will freeze over before his patrons can't enjoy a smoke. Unfortunately, the only free table is between a friendly looking, non-smoking couple with a cute baby who's sitting in a high chair munching on a prawn cracker, and a pair who look at you like something the dog just dropped when you sit down and put your cigarettes on the table. In my smoking days, the latter would have got me chain-smoking just for sport. But I couldn't do it to the couple with the baby and neither can you. So you try and enjoy your meal and pray they will leave soon so you can have an after-dinner cigarette. Bad luck. They don't, so you pay the bill and go. Once outside you gratefully light up and inhale deeply. You farewell your colleagues, catch your non-smoking bus/train/ferry/taxi home and probably have your last smoke of the day alone, in the dark in the backyard.

So what kind of day did you have? It wasn't brilliant, was it? In fact, you spent it as you spend most days – feeling anxious. Anxious about smoking. Anxious about finding opportunities to smoke, anxious even when you *are* able to smoke because you're doing it in such unrelaxed conditions. Anxious when the nicotine need slugs you and there's not a smoking opportunity in sight. Anxious because although you know the government's health campaigns have gone right over the top, you have been coughing a bit lately.

As well as feeling anxious you also feel resentful, angry even, because this small pleasure of yours – for which you are paying through the nose – has become so difficult to enjoy. At the same time as our great democracies have been outlawing discrimination of every kind, they've declared open season on smokers. And it's not likely to get better. In fact, while offering very little meaningful help to women who wish to give up – and that's most of us – those the government entrusts with the minuscule proportion of our tobacco taxes allocated to the health campaigns (currently around $2 million a year) are simply inventing new and more revoltingly graphic ways to tell you what you already know . . . that cigarette smoking is bad for you!

I feel sorry for smokers and I hate the government hypocrisy. They take all that revenue from smokers while encouraging others to harass and discriminate against them. It isn't fair. *Susan, 42, a smoker for 26 years, 20–25 a day. Hasn't smoked for 8 months.*

If only we'd stop trying

to be happy, we could

have a pretty good time.

EDITH WHARTON

3

Turning over
a new leaf

NICOTINE CAN PEP US UP, calm us down, aid concentration and help control hunger and body weight.
What a pity it isn't so clever at choosing the company it
keeps. On its own it could probably be of some benefit
to humankind, but while joined at the leaf by its constant companions, the 4000 or so chemicals contained
in each cigarette, it's an absolute dud of a recreational
drug. One day, no doubt, the boffins will come up with
a way of isolating it from those bad influences, where-
upon it will then be hailed as the latest wonder drug.
But for those of us who have been smoking for a few
years, that day is too far away for comfort. Much closer
to home is the very real prospect of becoming ill from
the effects of smoking.

This is the chapter in which those other quit-
smoking books might list all the horrible diseases and
other dire consequences of smoking. You won't find them
in this book. I decided to save time – mine and yours –
and trees, because I'm well aware that, like me, you are
so well acquainted with the health effects of smoking you

could recite them in your sleep. I asked my smokers and ex-smokers to list their reasons for wanting to give up smoking and every single one put health worries first, with lung cancer and emphysema named as the diseases that they'd least wish to become acquainted with. And I'm sure the most recent revelation, that smoking by women and passive smoking by girls may cause breast cancer, will give us all yet another reason to feel scared.

I hate everything about being a smoker. The smell, the taste, the worry of always needing to smoke, being a slave to an addiction, feeling socially stupid. But most of all, since I reached the age of 40, I've had a niggling fear that the next cigarette could be the one to trigger something awful like emphysema or lung cancer. *Olivia, 40, a smoker for 27 years, smokes 20–25 a day.*

I was sick of coughing and feeling lousy all the time. I wanted to play better tennis. I felt I wasn't in control of my life. Everything revolved around needing cigarettes. *Ann, 35, a smoker for 19 years, used to smoke up to 40 a day. Hasn't smoked for 22 months.*

I was worried about my health, especially my lungs – the wheezing. It was so filthy, the ashtrays stank, ash blows around, my teeth and fingers were stained. I was relating to non-smokers more than smokers. *Janey, 45, a smoker for 29 years, smoked 40–50 a day. Hasn't smoked for two and a half years.*

A fear of dying an ugly death. *Julie, 40, a smoker for 20 years, smoked 30–40 a day. Hasn't smoked for seven years.*

fear and loathing

The word 'fear' was used a number of times by both smokers and ex-smokers. It came up most often among the women aged from 35 onwards who have smoked since their teens and who are now very conscious of the physical effects of smoking, like coughing, shortness of breath and a recurring sore throat. Smokers and ex-smokers of all ages also noted how smoking is responsible for low energy levels – the word 'lethargy' came up several times.

I hated every aspect of smoking. I had started to notice a lethargic and unmotivated behaviour among older, long-term smokers that bordered on depression. I didn't want to become like that. *Justine, 32, a smoker for 13 years, smoked 20 a day. Hasn't smoked for 18 months.*

The term 'lack of control' was another used time and again by smokers. And 'regaining control of my life' and 'being free' were listed as two of the many highlights of success because, for heavy smokers who are honest with ourselves, there is no question of who – or rather, what – is in charge of things. It was only when

I stopped smoking that I admitted to myself just how lacking in control I had been. Since I would become acutely uncomfortable after more than two hours without a cigarette, nicotine controlled my choice of friends and acquaintances (few were non-smokers) and how I spent my leisure time; I would avoid places where smoking was not allowed or where I was likely to be asked not to smoke, such as people's homes, museums, art galleries, playgroup, indoor swimming pools. When I couldn't avoid these places, I'd be continually distracted by thoughts of smoking and get the hell out of the place as soon as I could.

Smoking also controlled my behaviour. One example of this still causes me to hang my head in shame. On a non-smoking flight from Hamilton Island to Sydney, the pilot announced – mid-flight – that we would be diverting briefly to Brisbane. Normally this journey would take two and a quarter hours, plus around 30 minutes to get through the airport. So having psyched myself into not smoking for three hours, the pilot's announcement threw me into a panic. Then I thought 'Hang on . . . airport, open space, a bar, a drink . . . a cigarette. This might not be so bad after all.'

Inside the airport, the No Smoking signs were all around until, as we approached the bar, I spotted a cigarette machine. Bingo! Love you, Queensland! But it was just a cruel trick. My partner went to get the drinks and asked for an ashtray as there were none on the tables. 'You can't smoke in here,' the barman said.

When my partner pointed to the cigarette machine, he shook his head sadly. 'We've only just gone non-smoking. That thing is driving people crazy. They should get rid of it.' Then, observing me wild-eyed, furious and doing my 'Smoking is a human rights issue' speech to the general populace of the bar, the sympathetic barman issued me with an empty beer can, and pointed towards a wide pillar at the far side of the bar area. I dashed off in that direction, and lurking behind the pillar was a pathetic group of other desperados all clutching their surrogate ashtrays and puffing like crazy in the hope of getting enough nico-tine into themselves before airport security spotted the clouds of smoke billowing out. I smoked two ciga-rettes in quick succession and started to calm down. But not before my partner had threatened to leave me in Brisbane if I didn't stop ranting and using the f-word at 98 decibels. Had I been a toddler, my behav-iour would have been called a tantrum! I dread to think what would have happened had it not been for that understanding barman.

To my mind, if women have gained anything posi-tive at all from the bully-boy tactics being employed against smokers, it's that the increasing day-to-day restrictions on when and where we can smoke have highlighted the strength of nicotine's grip. Once the hit from that last cigarette has worn off, which only takes between 40 minutes and an hour, our bodies start ask-ing for more. And that need for nicotine will dominate

whatever else is going on in our lives until it can be satisfied by a fresh supply. That puts us out of control in a
very big way.

Even light smokers, those who regularly smoke
only a few cigarettes a day, are being controlled by nicotine more than they may realise. I know people who
smoke perhaps four or five cigarettes a day and who
don't have their first until the evening. 'I'm not
addicted. I don't even think about it all day,' they say.
Most heavy smokers question why people who can
smoke only a few a day bother to smoke at all. The reason is that those few cigarettes a day are just as vital to
their equilibrium as the pack a day is for the dedicated
smoker. Otherwise, really, why bother?

The same goes for those irritating 'social' smokers
who, while never actually buying cigarettes, manage
to maintain a regular habit thanks to the generosity of
the paying puffer. They, too, may only be smoking a
few cigarettes a day, but next time you're in the company of one, see how they twitch and shuffle before
finally plucking up the courage to bludge one of yours.
If you wanted to have some fun you could try saying
no. But most smokers are far too kind-hearted to
refuse a cigarette to a fellow addict, even one in
denial. The fact is, those social smokers are not loath-
some people at all; it's their *need* for nicotine that is
controlling their behaviour. I'm sure most of them
would be only too happy to shout you a coffee or a
beer but I guess they feel that just so long as they don't

buy cigarettes, they can tell themselves they are not really smokers.

money for old rope

Of the secondary reasons given by smokers and ex-smokers for wanting to stop, the scent of a cigarette ranked high on the list, especially bad breath, smelly hair and clothes and the pong from dirty ashtrays. So too did being tired of the addiction and the inconvenience of needing to smoke. As for the ever-increasing price of a pack of cigarettes, only 22 per cent of smokers mentioned cost at all and even then it was seen as less important than health, bad breath and the sheer nuisance of smoking. Likewise, for the ex-smokers, financial cost wasn't an issue. Not one respondent cited this as a reason for, or a benefit of, giving up. Surprising, really, when you consider that at today's prices, shedding your average pack-a-day addiction could put up to $50 a week back in your wallet.

Health lobbyists such as the AMA are committed to the idea that whacking up the price of a packet of cigs is a potent motivator for people to stop, and they can produce a truckload of studies to prove their point. But that wasn't the message I got from my modest study. Perhaps price rises may be a major motivator for those who are not heavily addicted. They may also restrict the quantity of cigarettes smoked by the young who have limited funds, especially those still dependent on pocket money: I could make a pack of 20 last a week before I started working full-time at the age of 16. But cost alone does not stop us smoking. Once employed, I was still frequently strapped for cash and I'd moan and groan about every rise in the price of a pack of cigarettes. But rather than giving up I'd either switch to a cheaper brand or go without something else, including food, in order to keep buying cigarettes.

I think gender differences play a part here too. The males I know are very conscious of how much money they are saving by not smoking and are quite focused about redirecting it more profitably for themselves. Which I reckon is exactly the right thing to do! But women don't do this, do we? What usually happens when women give up smoking is that we buy ourselves the odd treat initially, then all those dollars we're saving become absorbed into the general household income. Or we buy treats for the kids. Later in the book I hope to persuade you to take a leaf out of the male manual, and make the money you are going to be saving one of the many visible long-term benefits of giving up smoking.

social insecurity

All smokers are sensitive to current social and political attitudes towards them, and to be socially acceptable was frequently given as a reason to stop smoking. Most smokers seem resigned to today's many restrictions on their freedom to smoke and only a few had a problem with being unable to smoke at work, in public buildings and on public transport. But the questions 'Do you find yourself frequently having to separate from a social group in order to smoke?' and 'If so, how does that make you feel?' clearly touched a raw nerve. Some 88 per cent answered yes to the first question, and in describing how this made them feel, 'angry', 'resentful', 'like a social pariah', 'an outcast' came bursting forth time and again.

> **It makes me feel ill at ease, like a pariah. And I feel resentful when so-called 'social' smokers bludge cigarettes.** *Bev, 51, a smoker for 32 years, smokes 25 a day.*

> **Like an alien, isolated, antisocial, frustrated, angry, an outcast.** *Chris, 36, a smoker for 20 years, smokes 20–25 a day.*

The question 'How do you feel about current social and political attitudes towards smokers?' produced a similarly hot response from the smokers . . . and a surprising amount of sympathy from the ex-smokers. Surprising considering three-quarters of ex-smokers admitted that since quitting, they now feel uncomfortable around people who are smoking, and consciously avoid smoky environments if they can. But the message that came across loud and clear was that although smokers are angry and resentful about the harassment and discrimination they suffer for indulging in what is, after all, a perfectly legal pastime, their dearest wish was to be non-smokers.

> **I think attitudes about having a smoke-free environment are really good. But they still come down a bit heavy-handed on those of us who do smoke.** *Paula, 25, a smoker for 8 years, smokes 15–25 a day.*

> **It makes me angry. I particularly detest passive–aggressive ex-smokers who cough and splutter and wave their hands in front of their noses when they're near you. I hate being told not to smoke in their self-righteous way, especially when they are drinking alcohol. I find alcoholic behaviour unacceptable but society accepts this.** *Angel, 34, a smoker for 15 years, smokes up to 50 a day.*

> **Smoking is filthy, disgusting, smelly and expensive. People like me should stop it immediately and prevent further damage to the air, other people and themselves.** *Sandi, 45, a smoker for 31 years, smokes 20–25 a day.*

In other words, you folk who are responsible for the quit campaigns, what we're trying to say is WE'VE HEARD YOU AND WE'VE GOT THE MESSAGE LOUD AND CLEAR! NOW COULD SOMEONE PLEASE LISTEN TO US?

I have my moments and

they are all weak ones.

MAE WEST

4

A campaign out of puff

CRAVINGS, STOMACH CRAMPS, dizziness, mouth ulcers, sweating, sleep disturbance, lack of concentration, anger, mood swings, weepiness, irritability, anxiety . . .

This sounds like a list of symptoms one might experience when withdrawing from a drug, such as a major tranquilliser, or an illegal drug like heroin. That's because it is. Nicotine is a powerful and addictive drug. Furthermore, women are more likely than men to experience some or all of these difficult symptoms when we attempt to give up smoking. Add to this the fear of putting on weight, plus the fear of failure and of not being able to live without cigarettes, and you have a straightforward explanation as to why, when smoking rates among males have been steadily declining over the past three decades, the rates for women have hardly changed at all. And although evidence of these gender differences has been around for some time, our quit campaigns have yet to take them into account.

How long does it take for a truckload of pennies to drop? Way back in 1980, the US Surgeon General's office had been busy collecting data on women and smoking from around the world and concluded that across the various quit-smoking methods, women had more difficulty than men giving up. One US scientist, who had been studying smoking and nicotine since 1979 and had drawn the same conclusion, was Neil Grunberg, Professor of Medical and Clinical Psychology and Neuro-science at the University of Health Sciences in Maryland. Between 1982 and 1985, Grunberg published a series of papers and conducted controlled animal experiments which showed clear evidence of a difference in the brain patterns of males and females. Then in the late 1980s and 1990s other scientists replicated his work by studying the effects of drugs, including nicotine, on the human population.

'We know that females are more sensitive than males to the physiological actions of nicotine,' Grunberg says. 'As a result, I believe that women generally have greater trouble quitting smoking and what's interesting is that women appear also to be less responsive to nicotine replacement therapy. I think every major conference on tobacco in the US currently acknowledges the importance of gender differences but the knowledge has not generally been incorporated into smoking cessation programs.' Ditto Australia.

It's been well documented that nicotine alters certain chemicals in the body, such as serotonin, the 'happy hormone'. Which goes some way to explaining why, when we stop smoking, we may feel like we're on an

emotional roller coaster. Again, these withdrawal symptoms are generally more pronounced in women than
they are in men. 'It's largely anecdotal but I think it's true
and, here, your or other people's anecdotes are as good
as mine,' Grunberg says. 'Women report greater problems with depression, they feel lousy, their moods are
affected. They experience a stronger craving for the drug
and are more likely to be affected by cravings for food
and body-weight changes.' He could have been talking
about me. And the majority of my respondents.

too much food for thought

As well as tinkering with the happy hormones, nicotine
reacts with insulin, which controls blood sugar. This has
the effect of changing our preferences for certain foods,
like sweet things and carbohydrates. Nicotine can suppress appetite, turn off a sweet tooth and speed up your
metabolism. And when you quit smoking? Back comes
that sweet tooth – and your metabolism goes into freefall.

The relationship between weight and nicotine is covered in detail in Chapter 7 – as is the reason why *you*
won't be putting on any weight in the first place. But the
subject deserves a mention here too, because fear of
weight gain is, according to Grunberg, the primary
reason why women and girls are still smoking. And he
should know. Although cigarettes have long been known
to control body weight, Grunberg was the scientist who
first isolated nicotine as chief of operations.

Around the time the good professor and his peers in the US were finding scientific reasons why intelligent, educated women in the Western world were having problems giving up smoking, across the Atlantic in the UK, medico and feminist Dr Bobbie Jacobson was also looking to the social order to provide some answers. And she found plenty, which she shares in two very readable studies on women and smoking – *The Lady-killers* (Pluto Press, 1981) and *Beating the Ladykillers* (Pluto Press, 1986).

It was in the late 1970s, while working for Britain's Action on Smoking and Health (ASH), which as well as collecting data on smoking also deals directly with smokers wishing to quit, that Jacobson, herself an ex-smoker, began to notice a pattern in the phone calls they were receiving: about three-quarters of the pleas for help were from women. But her path to discovering why was littered with obstacles. In the introduction to *The Ladykillers* she writes: 'Many experts on smoking and health met my questions about women smokers with sheer evasion and even defensiveness bordering on acrimony. Health educators and researchers do not normally study sex differences in smoking patterns, nor do they consult women when planning campaigns directed at women smokers, having assumed that what works for men will work for women.' She continues: 'I was even more disturbed by the lack of priority that women's organisations – feminist or otherwise – gave to the problem. A few expressed mild interest but most considered it to be strictly a non-issue.'

To the list of uninterested organisations I'd add
women's magazines. I don't wish to bite the hand that
fed me for so many years. As a magazine junkie from
early childhood, I was proud to work in a medium that
can entertain us with the lighter side of life – fashion,
celebrity news and gossip – and at the same time
empower us with information on a wide variety of
health issues all presented in an accessible way. I think
we have a lot to thank women's magazines for. I just
wish I knew why this outspoken industry has paid only
lip service to the very important women's health issue
of smoking and, in particular, to the difficulties many of
us face when we give up.

These days, the only quit-smoking articles you're
likely to see come once a year to coincide with World No
Smoking Day. Here is some typical advice: throw away
your cigarettes; keep a stock of raw vegetables in the
fridge for when you get the munchies, because you must
resist the urge to reach for the lolly jar at all costs; join
a gym to control your weight; when the urge to smoke
strikes, find something else to do with your hands; and
if you feel irritable, go for a walk. Accompanying these
lighter-than-light how-tos are photographs and 'case his-
tories' of radiant quitters who: a) have only quit the
week before the interview so they haven't had time to
put on any weight; b) have been going to the gym since
babyhood; c) are usually under 30; and d) always say
something like 'It was a bit tough for a day or two but
now it feels so wonderful to be a non-smoker!' I would

like to hear just one owning up to eating a family-sized bag of chips or block of chocolate in one sitting, and/or getting overwhelming urges to choke the living daylights out of someone who has done them no harm at all. Oh, and I would like to see an update on these 'success' stories a few months later.

In Australia, I'm told both male and female health professionals are involved in policy-making for the quit campaigns, which is why it is doubly depressing to note that the gender differences are still not taken seriously. The overriding philosophy of the campaigns is still to bully women into giving up smoking by generating as much fear and guilt (Smoking will harm your baby; Smoking kills; Your smoking harms others) as possible.

That anyone believes this campaign of terror can be truly effective is incredible. Another well-documented difference between the sexes is that women and men smoke differently. Jacobson's research showed that women tend to smoke when under emotional pressure, whereas men prefer to do so in relaxed or neutral circumstances. Men smoke to enhance a good feeling, while women are more likely to light up in order to smother an unwanted feeling, especially a socially diffi-cult one like anger or sadness or guilt or fear. Jacobson cites self-confidence as another difference between the sexes. Men, she says, commonly over-estimate their ability to accomplish a particular task, 'an attitude which acts to maximise their performance . . . Women, on the other hand, are great self-doubters. Men frequently say "I can give up any time I like", not a phrase commonly uttered by women.'

You don't have to look far to find evidence that men give up smoking more easily than women. We all know a male relative, a loved one, a loathed one, a friend, partner, colleague who one day decides enough is enough – he is giving up smoking. And he does. The chances are he'll go cold turkey. He won't waste money on nicotine replacements or other namby-pamby methods, and he wouldn't be seen dead reading a self-help book. He won't spend weeks analysing his decision either; hell, he probably won't even bother to boast about it. He'll just throw away his smoking equipment, buy a jar of sweets, be a bit short-tempered for a week or two, and emerge a non-smoker. How many women do you know who have done the same thing? None? Me neither.

> **For me it was a drug that would wake me up and put me to sleep. I was never alone with a cigarette. It was my friend. It took the edge off my intense feelings and helped me be confident. When I was hungry and had no food I could still smoke. It was a multi-purpose, go anywhere drug.** *Julie, 40, a smoker for 20 years, used to smoke 25 'real' cigarettes (15 mg) a day.*

Women often refer to cigarettes as a crutch, so what do you get when you take it away? Cravings, stomach cramps, dizziness, mouth ulcers, sweating, sleep disturbance, lack of concentration, anger, mood swings,

weepiness, depression, irritability . . . the sort of symptoms suffered by someone withdrawing from heroin.
But that's where the similarities end.

Unlike someone addicted to nicotine, a heroin
addict will only experience some of these symptoms and
she'll be over the physical ones in 72 hours. Whatever
the reality of withdrawing from heroin may be (and
those of us who have never experienced it can only
guess), nobody expects an addict to withdraw from
heroin and function normally at the same time. Yet,
while experiencing some or all of these symptoms –
acutely for at least ten days – the poor smoker is
expected to carry on regardless: get up, go to work, go
to the supermarket, look after the kids, cook dinner
AND not mind too much when someone wafts the drug
she is withdrawing from, *and craving*, right under her
nose. In other words, in spite of the fact that nicotine is
medically acknowledged as a drug that hooks users in
much the same way as heroin, smokers are expected to
stop smoking without their lives missing a beat.

Nicotine is being constantly compared with heroin
by both medics and media alike so I'm going to hold
that thought, especially as most smokers would ruefully
agree that their social status these days is on a par with
our stereotypical image of a hapless heroin addict. It's
been estimated that heroin-related crime costs our community $1.6 billion per year, and yet this destructive
drug contributes not one legitimate cent towards its
keep. In contrast, smokers fork out $4.6 billion a year

in tobacco taxes alone, of which only $2 million goes towards the quit campaigns. With one 1998 study putting the cost of caring for people who get sick at a mere $462 million per year, nicotine is a nice little earner for a government. Yet in an example of breathtaking hypocrisy, it pockets the money while at the same time playing the role of cheering spectator as the benefactors of all that revenue are ostracised, harassed, discriminated against, then made to pay all over again when they try to kick their addiction.

Free or subsidised nicotine replacement therapy, and quit programs which acknowledge the realities of nicotine withdrawal instead of trivialising them, were just two changes my smokers said they would like to see in future campaigns. A couple of respondents even suggested subsidised residential 'detox' centres which would free smokers from their day-to-day responsibilities while they learnt to live without nicotine. When you consider what smokers are putting into the community, I don't think that's a big ask.

As a breast-feeding

mother you are basically

meals on heels.

KATHY LETTE

5

Pregnancy – the mother of all incentives

ANOTHER MAJOR REASON for women wanting to give up smoking is the desire to get pregnant. Of my respondents, 32 per cent listed this as their first reason for wanting to quit – ahead even of concern for their own health. Yet, according to the Australian Medical Association (AMA), between one in three and one in four women in Australia smokes during pregnancy. And if you are one of those women, here's what one leading light in the anti-smoking campaign thinks of smokers in general: 'Being a smoker these days is almost a badge of lack of education or low social class,' he said. So now we know.

> **I felt really bad about smoking when I was pregnant. I cut down to a few a day, sometimes five or less, but I still felt terrible. I don't let the children see me smoke. My husband doesn't like me smoking, but he's a sweetie – he doesn't nag me too much . . . I've tried loads of times to give up and I just can't . . .** *Sonia, marketing consultant, tertiary-educated mother of three. Smokes 8–10 a day.*

How can they? bleat the media, the quit campaigners, the doctors and everyone else who feels entitled to share their opinion on this highly emotive subject. Don't these women know the terrible things that smoking does to unborn babies? Well yes, of course we do. Contrary to expert opinion, we're not stupid, even those of us who didn't come from nice middle-class families or attend private school and/or university. We all know we shouldn't smoke while we're pregnant or breast-feeding. Or anywhere near young children. What we also know is that the experts are not being entirely honest with us. Because they know very well that while maternal smoking has been linked to, among other things, miscarriage, low birth weight, infant respiratory problems and Sudden Infant Death Syndrome (SIDS or cot death), it is only *one factor* involved here. Other potent risks are poor nutrition, poverty, and a host of other social problems.

The fact is, intelligent, health-conscious, nurturing women do *not* damage their unborn babies *simply* by smoking cigarettes. Again I ask, how does distorting the truth or exaggerating the dangers of smoking help us break our addiction to nicotine? The answer is that it doesn't. It simply creates the kind of anxiety and guilt that causes us to reach for a cigarette in the first place. At the same time, it makes us feel cynical and gives us good reason to suspect a hidden agenda behind each new health warning, and to question the truthfulness of each shock-horror statistic. Such as the one I saw on a

commercial television network's early evening news
bulletin in May 1999: 'Women are taking up smoking
in pregnancy in order to reduce the size of their babies,'
the newsreader announced breathlessly. Not one shred
of evidence, not one single expert was produced to back
up such a claim . . . because there was none to be had.
It is simply not true.

This ridiculous story can be traced back to the
AMA's 1998 conference on smoking and pregnancy, at
which a female obstetrician presented anecdotal evidence of how apprehensive women are about giving
birth. (Now there's a surprise!) What this medic report-
edly said was: 'Some patients regard smoking as a way
of making their babies smaller so that delivery will be
easier.' What she appears to me to be suggesting is that
pregnant smokers, who find we can't quit, might think:
'Oh, well, at least I'll have a small baby and the birth
might not hurt so much.' It sounds like the kind of nervous joke we might make at an antenatal visit . . . one
we'd instantly regret when the doctor fails to get it. But
this doctor certainly did *not* say, as the news report
claimed, that women are 'taking up' smoking in pregnancy specifically to reduce the size of their babies. Yet
I didn't see this outrageous piece of misinformation
being publicly corrected by any of the usual vocal anti-
smoking mouthpieces.

further confessions of a reformed smoker

At the age of 38, after a planned, happy and trouble-free pregnancy, I gave birth to my first child – a beautiful, perfect baby boy, who arrived at 38 weeks, in just under four hours, in a birthing centre with no white coats or uniforms, no drugs and no complications. And he was born in the rudest of health, thank you very much, a happy state in which he remains to this day.

Of course I'm not proud that I smoked during pregnancy. I'm embarrassed and ashamed. But mostly I'm astonished. Because I'd wheezed my way through life convinced that pregnancy would be the one thing – probably the only thing – that would make me stop smoking. And for a while it was looking good. Seconds after the pregnancy was confirmed I threw away almost a full carton of fags and assorted lighters, and consigned all the ashtrays to a long-overdue retirement among the dust balls on top of the kitchen cupboard. *Nobody* would be allowed to smoke around my baby. And, thinking that giving away a glass or two of wine with dinner each night was going to be my biggest sacrifice for this brand new person, I tossed my industrial-strength corkscrew up there as well.

How wrong can you be? Within hours of the strip turning blue on the home pregnancy testing kit, my body was saying no to alcohol, coffee, red meat, spicy foods and all my other small pleasures in life, and yes to things I wouldn't normally touch with a very long ladle. Porridge, for instance, a gooey substance I survived numerous years of English winters without touching, and enough fresh fruit, vegetables, brown rice and legumes to give the average health freak multiple orgasms.

But my need for nicotine stayed as strong as ever. I managed to cut down while I was pregnant. The combination of guilt, shame, a non-smoking workplace, the absence of a cigarette's best pal – alcohol – plus being unable to stay awake past eight o'clock in the evening, ensured it. But I was still puffing away when my contractions were less than two minutes apart.

So what effect did my smoking have on my child? My baby son weighed 2.51 kilograms (5½ pounds) at birth. Does that make him a low birth-weight baby? The hospital thought so. Apparently, he was 'borderline'. Their bottom line was 2.50 kilos so he was actually .01 of a kilo *above* their 'textbook' healthy weight. Does the mother smoke? Yes. Oh, right. That explains everything. At the time, they were conducting a study into maternal smoking and low birth weight using data collected from the babies born in their hospital that year. So I'm sure we helped prove their point. But had they thought to seek either my consent to be studied – I first learnt of it from newspaper cuttings while researching this book – or my family history, they might have concluded that it was nature, not nicotine, that dictated my son's birth weight.

Like all the women on the maternal side of my family, I have a very small frame. I am 149 centimetres (4 feet 11 inches) short. My pre-pregnancy weight was around

47 kilos (7½ stone). I, myself, weighed 2 kilograms (5 pounds) at birth. My mother, who didn't smoke while she was pregnant with me, is 148 centimetres (4 feet 10 inches) short and has weighed less than 45 kilos (around 7 stone) for most of her life. Get the picture?

Nevertheless, without knowing all that, medical person or persons unseen used the knowledge that I smoked during pregnancy to justify removing my newborn baby from the tranquillity of the hospital's friendly, self-contained birth centre to the 'special care' nursery housed in one wing of the main hospital, while his sore and baffled mother languished in a chaotic post-natal ward in an adjoining building. Despite being stitched from ear to ear, for 48 hours I traipsed back and forth between the buildings half a dozen times a day. Meanwhile, my gorgeous baby lay in that impersonal high-tech room in a regular no-tech hospital cot, free of tubes, rosy-cheeked, placid, alert, looking like a miniature bodybuilder compared with most of the poor little scraps in there. Whenever I asked someone in a white coat what my baby was doing there, they'd mutter something about low birth weight and low blood sugar and rush away.

Even though I knew instinctively that my baby was perfectly healthy – just as the mother of a newborn who is not healthy often knows something is wrong before the medics do – they were able to get away with separating us because I was guilty as charged. I smoked during pregnancy. But for that, I would have been screaming blue murder the moment they took him away from me.

So what if I hadn't smoked in pregnancy and my son had still been a borderline 'textbook' weight? Would they have listened to what I had to say? 'Probably', says one midwife friend. 'Definitely', says another. 'Maybe', says a GP. We'll never know.

Compared with what some new parents suffer at the hands of an inflexible health-care system, this was nothing. And I had oodles of moral support from others among the hospital staff . . . all of it off the record, mind you. Because such is the status of smokers and smoking these days that nobody is going to stick their neck out to support you for fear of getting their head chopped off.

So if you are planning to be pregnant please, please try to give away cigarettes at least three months before you throw out your contraception. And do it for *your own* sake – not just for your baby's, not for your partner, certainly not just because your doctor tells you to. Do it for yourself. First-time motherhood is a high like no other, but it makes us vulnerable to all sorts of nonsense. When you have a baby you are suddenly surrounded by experts everywhere you go . . . like in the street, or in a shop, or at a barbecue. This type rarely has any medical training, some have never even given birth, and some gave birth in the days when there were only two ways to parent: a 'right' way and a 'wrong' way. These 'experts' are often complete strangers, their advice unsolicited, often inappropriate and occasionally downright spiteful. Like the elderly woman who spotted a new mum enjoying a quiet moment in a coffee shop, her baby sleeping peacefully in a stroller by her side. 'You shouldn't be sitting in here on a nice day like this,' she said crossly. 'That poor baby should be in the park getting some fresh air.' Or the busybody, young enough to know better, who told a 41-year-old new mum that she had 'no right' to have a baby 'at your age because you'll be too old to babysit your grandchildren'. Though tactless, old-fashioned and ill-informed, comments like these can press guilt buttons and shake your confidence in a very big way. Giving up smoking does wonders for your confidence, and gives you one less reason to feel guilty.

I found no reputable data on the success rate of women who try to give up smoking after becoming pregnant. I deliberately didn't ask about smoking in pregnancy in my questionnaires because I thought it could be seen as hostile by the many, many women who responded to my survey who didn't know me from Adam, or how my research was going to be used. But anecdotal evidence suggests that most women who smoke in pregnancy learn the hard way, just as I did, that pregnancy is not a reliable form of aversion therapy. Neither is guilt, otherwise I don't believe any woman would smoke in pregnancy.

As yet, we can't even turn to nicotine substitutes for help: currently aids such as the patches or gum are not recommended for use in pregnancy. How logical is that? I don't see how measured doses of nicotine delivered through the mother's skin can be more harmful to a growing foetus, or to the mother, than the nicotine delivered in cigarettes, via smoke into the lungs, accompanied by 4000 chemicals. Amazingly, even some Australian medics agree with me on this one. One of the recommendations at the AMA's 1998 conference on pregnancy and smoking was that this issue should be re-examined. At the time of writing, this still hasn't happened. But we live in hope. Meanwhile, anecdotal evidence suggests that even those women who do find the willpower to stop for the duration of a pregnancy usually start smoking again soon after the baby is born. And those of us with smoking partners are particularly vulnerable. The truth is, failing to keep cigarette smoke away from babies – unborn or otherwise – will lead you on the guilt trip of a lifetime when all you really want to do is sleep!

It will be of some consolation to women to know that the quit campaigners have at last realised it takes two to make a baby, and consequently set their malevolent sights on smoking dads as well. While smoking mothers are charged with causing all manner of ills to the unborn child, smoking fathers are being hit with the big C. Men who smoke at the time of conception, says the Cancer Council, cause their babies to develop cancer in later life because the poisons in tobacco affect the sperm causing gene mutations which in turn cause cancer.

Not as grim, but not good news for the male of the species, is the claim from some boffins in Boston,

Massachusetts, that men who smoke have smaller erec-
tions. This lot reckon that because smoking damages
the blood vessels and inhibits the blood flow, it also
affects elastin, the substance believed to govern a man's
ability to have an erection. With the health warnings
about smoking getting wilder by the day, it's easy to
sneer at a story like this. But it's one of those nuggets
that can sometimes niggle away at you because, damn
it, there's always a chance it could be true. In this case,
according to Neil Grunberg, there is much evidence to
show it *is* true. Perhaps they could add it to the warnings on the packs: 'Warning – Cigarettes Can Reduce
Your Erection!'

To cease smoking is the easiest thing I ever did . . . I've done it a thousand times.

MARK TWAIN

6

If she can do it, anyone can!

OF THE EX-SMOKERS WHO took part in my survey, nearly all reported that they had tried in the past to quit with varying degrees of success. It was 'third time lucky' for me, and the third attempt was also a winner for 46 per cent of my ex-smokers. Meanwhile, a significant 40 per cent hit the jackpot on their second attempt. Just 12 per cent reported three or more failed attempts, with one brave soul admitting it took her ten tries before she finally succeeded.

The point is, she *did* succeed. And you will too. I asked all the ex-smokers why they thought those past attempts had failed, and around half gave lack of motivation as the reason. Of the rest, the break-up of a relationship proved a powerful trigger to reach for that old friend, as did the sheer ferocity of the withdrawal symptoms. Weight gain caused a number of them to light up again and, sadly, several, one of whom hadn't smoked for two years, found out the hard way that 'Just one cigarette . . .' is a not a good idea. I discuss that nasty little pitfall later in the book.

My heart goes out particularly to Moyra, below, who stopped smoking for three years and then got herself re-addicted. Those of us whose past efforts only lasted a few weeks can get some fairly instant gratification once we beat our previous pathetic best. She's got a way to go to pass her previous fantastic best. But I bet she makes it, just as you will.

In the past, sure, I wanted to give up. But I wasn't really committed to the idea. This time, though, I'd reached the stage where I hated everything about smoking – the smell, the taste, the coughing, the sheer inconvenience of it all. And because of my age, I was also frightened. So, I guess you could say that this time around I was truly motivated. *Susan, 42, a smoker for 26 years, smoked 20–25 a day. Hasn't smoked for eight months. Quit on third attempt.*

I was successful for three years until a relationship broke up. Then, one puff and I was gone. *Moyra, 35, a smoker for 19 years, smoked 20–30 a day. Hasn't smoked this time for eight months.*

Like the ex-smokers, almost all of the smokers who responded to my survey had tried to stop in the past and all were able to succeed for at least a few weeks. And if you've managed to stop even for a few days or a few weeks, your next attempt could be the one that sets you free of the weed for good. Incidentally, the smokers who answered my survey who said they had never attempted to quit were all under the age of 25. And with all due respect to them, I have yet to meet anyone under 25 who regards their smoking as a serious health issue. They are likely to still be single, with no cough, probably no kids, no sense of being addicted, plus the ability to stay out all night drinking, smoking and generally abusing their bodies and still appear pink-cheeked and bushy-tailed the next day. I say enjoy it while you can, girls. There will come a time when those post-party cheeks will be tinged with grey, and as for the bushy tail – we're talking tail of drowned rat!

When we're in our early 20s it's hard to visualise anything much changing. But although we tend not to worry too much about the health effects of smoking, it interests me how many young women smokers have got 30 flagged as the age to quit. It seems it's a definite milestone age for women. 'I wanted to stop smoking before I was 30,' said Sophie who, at 27, decided to give herself a head start by making a serious attempt to quit. She stopped for eight months and then lapsed. Last I heard she was having another go and had made it to three months this time.

To all you other smart twentysomethings, I say why wait until the onset of 30 to take the plunge? As well as being a milestone age for women it's also when many of us start getting the jitters about health and wrinkles. Nowadays, too, your thoughts might be turning to having a baby . . . So if you're already motivated enough to set yourself a stop date, albeit several years ahead, why not think about doing it sooner? That way, not only will the withdrawal symptoms be more manageable, your body will reward you enormously when you get into your 30s and beyond. This is not a doctor talking, but one prematurely wrinkled ex-smoker who at 25 couldn't visualise turning 40! I enjoyed my 30s enormously but now I know how great it feels to be free of nicotine, I can't help wondering how much better life could have been had I given up smoking sooner.

age of reason . . . or is it panic?

While we know it's not easy for 25-year-olds to visualise being 40, and those of us who've reached it might wish it hadn't arrived so fast, the onset of maturity isn't all bad news. For a start, the older you are, the better your chances of quitting smoking for good. Of my group of ex-smokers, three-quarters are over 35, with the biggest age-group being the over-40s. For them, the old saying 'Life begins at 40' has turned out to be true.

If age is no barrier, neither is the length of time you've been smoking or how heavy a smoker you are. The majority of my triumphant quitters were women like me – highly addicted smokers who had not been free of cigarettes since childhood.

What I love best about being a non-smoker is glow-ing vibrant skin. Lots of people remarked how pink

my skin was becoming rather than grey. Then there's the fresh breath, clean hair, clothes, house – no stink of stale smoke. No aching lungs, no disapproving looks, no self-hatred. *Christine, 41, a smoker for 17 years, smoked 20–40 a day. Hasn't smoked for 18 months. Quit on second attempt.*

I have good lungs and I don't feel suicidal. I can smell and taste food and I don't wake up with a birdcage mouth. I don't have ashtrays smelling my house out. *Janey, 45, a smoker for 29 years, smoked 50–60 a day. Hasn't smoked for two and a half years. Quit on her third attempt.*

As for those past failed attempts at stopping? Consider them a learning curve, valuable training for your new life as a non-smoker. It makes sense when you think about it. If your last effort saw you stop smoking for three weeks, you now know what those first three weeks are going to be like. Not much fun, were they? But armed with the knowledge gained that time, this time you can take steps to make it easier on yourself. My first serious attempt to quit smoking lasted just five days. For me it was awful. I felt like I'd stepped onto another planet where everything had been speeded up and I couldn't keep pace. So when I was planning my second attempt, I knew I'd need some help. At the time, the only nicotine replacement therapy available was the gum, so I took it. That time I didn't smoke for four months, and it was an absolute miracle, the longest I'd been without a cigarette for 25 years. Okay, so I subsequently blew it, but the memories of how good it felt being a non-smoker helped keep me motivated during the next – and final – attempt.

In explaining the hold that cigarettes have on them, some of the women who responded to my survey hinted at a childhood trauma, while others were more specific, citing the loss of a parent, physical/emotional abuse, or sexuality issues as a reason for using cigarettes as a crutch. Once again, Bobbie Jacobson adds some empathy to this aspect. In *The Ladykillers*, she writes: 'Smoking is an outward sign of our constant battle to control our unvoiced frustrations; controlling these means we can be nice to everybody.'

Sadly, I don't think anything can ever truly right the wrongs of an unhappy childhood. When those who bring us into the world, or others who are responsible for our well-being as children, let us down badly – either wilfully or unwittingly – they leave us standing on very shaky ground indeed. Those experiences inevitably follow us into adulthood, and you don't need a degree in psychology to understand how nicotine, alcohol or other drugs that can suppress powerful feelings and make us feel better can, at least in the short term, wheedle their way into our lives and take over.

If you are a smoker and also suffering emotional problems that go back to childhood, you might benefit from some good-quality professional counselling. And it might even be worth setting that ball rolling before you set a date to stop smoking. Any positive help you get will increase your chances of getting free of nicotine. But I guarantee that giving up smoking will do more for your self-esteem and overall sense of well-being than a whole lifetime of counselling. Oh, and here's what else you'll be doing for yourself:

- Improving the blood flow around your body, making your skin look pinker, healthier and younger. In particular, you'll retard the development of those fine vertical lines above the mouth that are oh-so-ageing. (Some of us wish we'd stopped smoking before they appeared!)

- Making it safer to take the contraceptive pill, particularly if you are over 30.

- Improving your fertility and turning back your body clock. Because nicotine affects hormones, women who smoke may reach menopause before those who don't.

- Increasing your chances of having a healthy, guilt-free pregnancy.

- Reducing excess body hair. Don't laugh. Studies in the US cite this as another visible hormonal effect of smoking cigarettes, and I'm amazed it hasn't been taken up in Australia. I first read it in a British women's magazine in the 1980s. Pictured with the article was a chain-smoking character from the BBC soapie 'EastEnders' with a distinct moustache drawn on her top lip. I read it and fumed. Another 'let's make women feel anxious about smoking' statistic. But deep down I believed it. You see, along with cigarettes, another of my long-term expenses had been waxing – full leg, bikini, top lip, you name it. Since I stopped smoking, this painful chore has been reduced to legs only, just a few times a year instead of every four weeks.

■ Reducing your chances of getting any of those ghastly diseases like lung cancer, emphysema, chronic bronchitis, heart disease, stroke, gangrene, cancer of the fingernail (sorry, I couldn't help myself).

■ Awarding yourself a tax-free pay rise. At today's prices, a former pack-a-day smoker can look forward to a windfall of around $50 to $55 a week. That's $2600 a year!

When anorexics look

in the mirror

they see someone fat.

So I'm anorexic.

Jo Brand

7

Weighty matters

Nearly all women want to be thin. Being thin has a meaning for women that it does not have for men . . . [so] it is easy to see why [a woman] might believe that being thin is more important than stopping smoking. It's not that she doesn't recognise that smoking is far more damaging to her health than putting on weight but that she views controlling her weight as a more immediate priority. The thought of being fat, undesired and unsuccessful seems more difficult to face than the prospect of becoming ill from smoking at some undefined future date.

BOBBIE JACOBSON, *The Ladykillers*

While ramming home the health effects of smoking to almost ludicrous proportions, the quit campaigns have relegated the side-effects of giving up to a virtual non-issue. And none has had a heavier veil thrown over it than the issue of putting on weight. It's only recently that this very real side-effect of quitting smoking has been acknowledged at all. Yet the size of the gain for many, many women, and the impact that unwanted weight has on women and girls both emotionally and in terms of self-esteem, is largely being ignored.

One newspaper article published on World No Smoking Day 1999 illustrates this perfectly. While acknowledging nicotine as an appetite suppressant and admitting that when you stop smoking your metabolism slows down, the gender differences are not mentioned. Instead, the article trots out the oft-repeated 'statistic' that only one-third of those who quit smoking will put on weight, then quotes an 'expert' thus: 'Many people use nicotine as an appetite suppressant, although in terms of risk factor, they would be much better off putting on a little weight than smoking.' This master of the bleedin' obvious goes on to say that the change in metabolism is only half the reason why people gain weight after giving up cigarettes. 'People are eating under stress, and they are eating high-sugar, high-fat comfort foods,' he says. The advice? Throw away your cigarettes and prepare whole-some comfort food. *WHOLESOME* COMFORT FOOD! WHAT IS THAT EXACTLY?

Three-quarters of the women who answered my survey put on weight after quitting smoking. This ranged from 3–4.5 kilograms (7–10 pounds) to as much as 13 kilos (2 stone). I can personally vouch for 13 kilos because that's how much weight I put on. The gain became noticeable within about eight weeks of stopping smoking and I continued to pile on the kilos for at least

12 months. Yet I had stopped stuffing my face with 'high-sugar, high-fat comfort foods' within the first three to four months. Which doesn't surprise Neil Grunberg, who reckons it takes about a year for your metabolism to stabilise once you stop smoking.

At the time of writing my weight is back to a level I am comfortable with, but it was hard work and I'm still as mad as hell that I didn't know beforehand what was going on. In fact, I'm wondering who I can sue for the cost of all the 'fat clothes' I had to buy during my body's relentless, and unnecessary, expansion from a size 8 to a 14. And I wouldn't mind claiming a few thousand dollars for suffering and humiliation. Like the day I was crossing a road, obviously too slowly for the bozo in a BMW who was waiting to turn. He tooted at me and when I looked up I saw him mouth, 'Hurry up, you fat cow!' Only joking about suing but, really, weight gain is the only gain to be had by ignoring the evidence – both scientific and anecdotal – about nico-tine's most appealing side-effect.

Both women and men put on weight when they give up smoking. I once heard the Australian actor John Wood ('Blue Heelers') say in a TV interview that he had 'quit smoking and put on two stone straight away'. He seemed remarkably cheerful about it. But Jacobson is right: being thin *does* have a meaning for women that it does not have for most men. Nobody would suggest that men enjoy being overweight, but their sense of self-worth and self-confidence aren't so inextricably linked to their physical appearance as is the case with most women. I'm sure we all wish things were different, but for most of us it's a fact of life.

Not wanting to impose my body image hang-ups on others, I asked my ex-smokers, 'Was the weight gain a problem for you?' and got a resounding 'Yes!' from them all. When I asked, 'Which were the most difficult of all the withdrawal symptoms to overcome?', weight gain was number one by a mile; more than three-quarters of women put it at the top of the list. None of the other symptoms even came close. For the majority of those who had been smoke free for six months or longer, the weight problem was the *only* withdrawal symptom remaining.

That nicotine is a highly efficient means of con-trolling body weight and suppressing appetite has been well known anecdotally for at least a century. Or longer, according to Neil Grunberg, who says, 'This was cer-tainly known by the native American peoples who used to smoke or chew tobacco leaves.' In the 1920s the slo-gan 'Reach for a Lucky instead of a sweet' helped make Lucky Strike America's top-selling cigarette brand. Today, any teenage girl can tell you that the best way to stave off hunger pangs – and stay trim – is to smoke cigarettes. And there are sound scientific reasons why it works. Nicotine is a stimulant which, among other things, means it increases your body's metabolic rate – the rate at which it burns energy or kilojoules. In other words, someone who smokes, say, a pack of cigarettes a day, will invariably be able to consume more kilojoules per day than a non-smoker without gaining any weight.

So what happens when you deprive your body of nicotine? Exactly! Your metabolism slows down, leaving you with a load of extra kilojoules all dressed up with nowhere to go except to your stomach, thighs and hips. Your body may also convert more of the fat in your diet to body fat than it did when you smoked. And if that's not enough bad news, it is now known that nicotine alters the balance of particular chemicals in the body, including insulin which controls blood sugar, and serotonin, that so-called happy hormone, in the brain. Put into layperson's terms, Neil Grunberg says, 'The effect on the insulin, in particular, changes the preferences we have for different foods, like sweets and carbohydrates.'

Why this would affect women more than men is not really clear. 'We do not know the mechanism,' says Grunberg. 'However, we do know that women, as well as females of other species, are more sensitive to the actions of nicotine.' What's more important, though, is that when you throw away your cigarettes without knowing all this, what subsequently happens to your body is more or less out of your control. It's not good enough for the so-called 'experts' to assert that a few extra kilos in weight is better than getting lung cancer or emphysema. That's not how most women and girls see it. And as for the prevailing advice on how to deal with the weight, most of it defies belief. Here is an example: instead of reaching for the sweet jar or eating a plate of high-kilojoule pasta, keep the fridge stocked with low-kilojoule, low-fat snacks. Oh, and while you're at it, with all the money you're saving on ciga- rettes you could start going to the gym.

What's wrong with that advice? On the surface of it, nothing. But when you add even moderately flawed human beings to the equation, the answer is everything. Firstly, a handful of jelly beans or a delicious bowl of pasta are perfect cures for a nicotine craving. It takes an iron will to reach for a piece of raw carrot or a water biscuit when your body is craving sugar or carbohy- drate. Someone who is simply on a low-kilojoule diet can only keep that up for a short while. For those of us who are in the throes of nicotine withdrawal, it's just too big an ask. So is expecting someone to withdraw from nicotine and change their dietary habits at the same time. Throw in the advice to join a gym and what these sadists are suggesting you do is make three big lifestyle changes – quit smoking, go on a diet and start an exercise regime – all in one hit.

I know someone who gave up smoking and joined a gym on the same day. Up to that point the most exer- cise she had done since schooldays was running after her two small children. From the start, she spent several hours a day, six days a week in the gym. 'I'm an addic- tive personality,' she joked. 'I was once addicted to cigarettes and then I became a gym junkie.' She stayed off the cigarettes and these days she runs marathons. Did she put on weight after she stopped smoking? Of course she didn't! But spending two hours a day, six days a week in the gym is not an option for most women. What's more likely to happen when it all gets too hard is we will reach for a chocolate bar . . . or a cigarette!

Being caught unawares by the ferocity of the nicotine withdrawal symptoms is bad enough. But when you wake up one morning and discover that you really don't have anything to wear because nothing fits any more, the feel-good factor of quitting smoking can go right out of the window along with your self-esteem.

It depressed the hell out of me. I couldn't fit into any of my trousers and I couldn't afford new ones, so I had to grit my teeth and exercise. *Justine, 32, a smoker for 14 years, used to smoke 20 a day, up to 50 on a bad day. Hasn't smoked for 18 months. Gained 6.5 kilograms (1 stone).*

It affected how I would present myself. I lost a bit of confidence. I felt fat and ugly. I'm still trying to lose weight. *Anne, 32, a smoker for 20 years. Hasn't smoked for one year, seven months. Put on 13 kilograms (around 2 stone).*

You may find this hard to believe right now, but it is EASIER to give up smoking than it is to lose weight, especially a lot of weight and especially once you reach your 30s and 40s and onwards, that time in your life when you are most likely to be seriously wanting to get free of the weed. Unfortunately this is also a time when your body's metabolism is starting to slow down all by itself. Which is another compelling reason for giving up in your 20s. But the good news is that unlike me and all the women who took part in my survey, you don't have to worry about it because you will not be putting on the weight in the first place. Remember those delinquent kilojoules I talked about earlier? In the next chapter I explain how to send them on their way painlessly *and* well before you smoke your last cigarette.

Everything you see

I owe to spaghetti.

S O P H I A   L O R E N

8

Those kamikaze kilojoules – pack 'em off, not on!

IT'S OFTEN SAID it takes three weeks to break a bad habit, so it's reasonable to suppose you can entrench a good one in more or less the same time. But to be on the safe side, you could allow four weeks for the following minor adjustments to your daily routine to become so familiar that you don't have to think about them. Instead, you'll be able to concentrate on the big one – freeing yourself from nicotine with one major withdrawal symptom taken care of.

However, if four weeks aren't long enough, then extend the time. The object of this exercise is to see off those wayward kilojoules *before* you stop smoking, so that you are not being forced to do two difficult tasks at the same time: i.e. control your body weight and deal with your need for nicotine. So it is vital that you are feeling confident about the changes you've made before you set your quit date.

If possible, plan your quit campaign for spring or summer. Spring is symbolically a time for optimism and new beginnings. But as well as being a good time spiritually, it is also a very practical time to be starting your new life as a non-smoker. For one thing, the warmer weather encourages even the most slothful of us to be more active. And as the mercury rises, we tend to replace kilojoule/fat-heavy meals like roasts and casseroles and puddings with lighter ones like stir-fries, salads and fruit. In warmer weather, most of us natu-rally eat less anyway.

In his book *How To Stop Smoking Without Gaining Weight* (Bantam, 1995), US nutritional expert Dr Martin Katahn also takes the 'prevention is better than cure' approach by advising his readers to get their weight under control before quitting smoking. And Neil Grunberg wholeheartedly endorses this strategy. Katahn puts the number of rogue kilojoules rampaging around your body when you stop smoking at a minimum of 840 (200 calo-ries) per day. 'I think that's roughly true,' says Grunberg. 'But there is a tremendous amount of variance. As your readers will know, genetics and things such as diet and your level of exercise at the time of smoking cessation will affect your metabolic rate, as will any increase in the con-sumption of sweet or carbohydrate foods.'

However, he says, 840 kilojoules is a good ballpark figure and the number of ways you can find to disperse them each day are many and varied. The most painless way is to combine some moderate exercise with a moder-ate reduction in the fat content in your diet, because high-fat foods can easily convert to body fat and usually contain the highest number of kilojoules. Which is not to say that some low- or no-fat sugary foods – which you are likely to crave when you stop smoking – are not high in kilojoules, but they do not convert to body fat so easily.

More exercise does not mean sweating it out in a gym, unless that's your idea of fun; nor does eating less mean munching on raw vegetables while your body is screaming for sugar. Just literally moving around for 40 minutes more each day than you do now can save you 840 kilojoules. As will cutting 20 grams of fat a day from your diet. For instance, a brisk 20-minute walk (525 kjs/125 cals), plus leaving the butter and mayo off your lunch-time sandwich (571 kjs/136 cals), will see these rogues off for one day, with some to spare. Another day, you can enjoy your mayo, but do your brisk 20-minute walk with your toddler in the pram (781 kjs/186 cals). If you don't have kids, finding a hill or some stairs to sprint up and down will use up 780 kjs (185 cals). At the end of the book, you'll find a list of popular sports and everyday activities and how much energy they use.

If you are a fairly active person who plays sport or goes to the gym – or if you already keep an eye on the fat in your diet – you will find this simple strategy a breeze. If you are usually inactive, unsporty, gymophobic and find it hard to resist high-fat goodies like chips and chocolate for more than a few days at a time, it still shouldn't be difficult. For one thing you are highly motivated. You are about to become a non-smoker and you want to spend the money you will save on treats. You do not want to waste it buying bigger clothes to accommodate a load of extra weight. Piling on unwanted weight takes the shine right off the sense of achievement to be had from beating nicotine addiction.

The other reason I know you'll find it easy is because I did, and I am lazy, unsporty, gymophobic and not very good at self-denial. So if I can do this, so can you. Of course, I didn't have the necessary weight-management knowledge before I gave up smoking, so I wasn't able to stop it going on in the first place. Instead, I used a stricter version of this strategy to help me lose the weight I wanted (see Chapter 16) after the event.

And I guarantee it works. Even when I was smoking I had the world's slowest metabolism. The old saying 'what you eat today will be on your hips/bottom/thighs tomorrow' was my catch-cry. Being short – well, petite sounds nicer – a little goes a long way with me. In fact, it goes everywhere except the one place I wouldn't mind it. You know what I mean – it starts on the face, travels to the arms, then while somehow managing to avoid the A-cup breasts altogether, makes its way straight to the stomach and beyond. In my case, it goes from my arms to my stomach via my back. And it's a sad day for any woman who finds herself going up two bra sizes simply to accommodate a wider back.

move more

Exercise. I chose walking because I enjoy it and it's free – all you need are some comfortable old clothes and joggers or tennis shoes. I try to do a 45-minute brisk walk (999 kjs/238 cals) two or three times a week and, as I live in a hilly suburb, it's rewarding too as I can feel the muscles tugging with every incline. I use these walks as my quiet time, time alone to drift off into my head, to think about things, to work out how to tackle problems and make future plans. And I feel invigorated at the end of it.

Other than that I swim (incompetently) about once or twice a week (mostly in summer) for about 20 minutes (798 kjs/190 cals). Then there's all the usual domestic exercise like cleaning the house (243 kjs/58 cals for every 15 minutes), cooking dinner (180 kjs/43 cals) and playing ball with my son (197 kjs/47 cals). Using the stairs at work instead of the lift burns up 588 kjs (140 cals). And I started learning the piano recently – something I've wanted to do all my life – and have since found out this very pleasurable activity uses 159 kjs every 15 minutes. What a good excuse to practise! With the domestic chores though, don't forget that this exercise needs to be *in addition to* your normal activities. So if you usually cook dinner every night you can't count that one. Better to get your partner to cook dinner while you go for a nice walk!

Giving up smoking helps increase your energy. As a result, even sloths will want to become more active. Having gone out of my way to avoid physical activity for most of my adult life, I'm now enjoying the modest amount I am doing – and thinking about doing more, like playing one of the sports I was good at in school,

such as netball (432 kjs/103 cals every 15 minutes) or
badminton (300 kjs/71 cals). I still don't fancy the gym.
I went to one once. It was full of borderline anorexics
in pristine designer gym gear and over-upholstered jog-
ging shoes, resplendent in full make-up with not a bead
of sweat on their beautifully plucked brows. That I
could have coped with. What ensured I'd never darken
the establishment's doorstep again was its freezing-cold
indoor swimming pool (designed to keep inmates moving, I guess) and communal changing rooms full of
more borderline anorexics who stared in horror at anyone with more than one millimetre of flesh on her
bones.

eat less

We in the West are always being told our diets contain
too much fat, so this could be the perfect excuse to cut
some out without even noticing it's gone. The recommended healthy intake of fat for women who are not
looking to lose weight and who are moderately active
seems to vary, but most sources peg it at between 40 and
50 grams per day – or no more than 25 per cent of your
total energy (kilojoule/calorie) intake. But we do need fat
in our diet; the experts say you need at least 25 grams a
day even when trying to lose weight. I found the best
way to cut down on fat, without dying of boredom or
feeling sorry for myself, was to cut out – and cut down
on – the ones I don't care about (butter on bread, milk

in tea and coffee, oily dressing on salad, fatty meats and so on), keep a check on the ones I love (cheese, chocolate, chips, roast lamb, plus olive oil with everything), and give myself time off for good behaviour on weekends and special occasions.

getting started

If you haven't already got one, you'll need to invest in a fat counter from your local book store or newsagent. For around $5 each, the pocket-sized *Australian Fat, Fibre & Energy Counter* (by Julie Stafford, Penguin) and nutritionist Rosemary Stanton's *Fat & Fibre Counter* (Wilkinson Books) cover more or less every food and beverage you're likely to come across in Australia. And more and more food products obligingly have their fat and kilojoule content shown on the packaging.

Next choose three gastronomically unremarkable days in your life and write down everything that passes your lips. Look up the fat content, write the figure next to the food and add up each day's total. Take the middle total as your daily average, then start looking at where you might be able to save. Every 20 grams of fat you can cut from your diet will put you 756 kilojoules (180 calories) a day in credit. If you've never bothered to record your food intake in this way before, you might want to do it for longer, just for sport. I did it for a few weeks while I was researching my chapter on losing weight after quitting, and I found it interesting to discover which foods were sending my daily fat and kilojoule limits through the roof. I truly didn't know any of this because thanks to nicotine, I hadn't needed to kilojoule count for years.

The other benefit of that little monitoring exercise was to show me that my daily fibre intake was woefully low. To be honest, until I started this project I didn't know the recommend daily intake of anything. I wasn't interested enough in food to find out. Yet as a sub-editor on various women's magazines I must have read all this stuff all the time – it's just that the mechanics of it never sank in because I didn't see what it had to do with me. But I was wrong and for anyone who doesn't know, the recommended daily dose of fibre is 25 to 30 grams.

That's it. That's all you need to know in order to get those kamikaze kilojoules under control. Take three or four weeks – or as long as you need – to get this simple strategy so firmly fixed into your routine that you can't remember doing anything different. Then you're ready to move on and look at how best to achieve your main goal – to free yourself from cigarettes.

I generally avoid

temptation, unless

I can't resist it.

MAE WEST

How addicted are you? Have fun finding out

THIS IS THE POINT where most stop-smoking guides advise you to assess your level of nicotine dependency before deciding how much help, if any, you'll need to give up. Some even set you little quizzes to do, like the ones you sometimes find in the magazines – How Good Is Your Sex Life? If you answered mainly As, you are a nymphomaniac; mainly Bs, you are normal to boring; mainly Cs, the convent is down the road and turn left.

I'm sure most of you know how addicted you are to nicotine. Lighting up in the street in all weathers after a couple of hours in the cinema is a dead give-away. So, too, is needing sedation when you run out of cigs and the shops are shut. But most of us enjoy a good quiz. So here's my very own version of How Addicted Are You?

QUIZ

1. When you wake up in the morning what's the first thing you do?

a) Grope around on the floor beside your bed for a cigarette and smoke it before you open your eyes.

b) Get up, go for a pee, put the kettle on, then grope around among last night's mess for your cigarettes.

c) Get up, pee, shower, have coffee/breakfast, go to work, and only around mid-morning do you allow yourself to have your first – and second – cigarette of the day.

2. You're going cold turkey and you haven't smoked for two days. You go to the supermarket. When you reach the checkout, the operator serves the previous customer then, ignoring you, she/he unhurriedly begins unwrapping coin packs and dispensing them into the cash register. How does this make you feel?

a) Calmly, cold-bloodedly murderous.

b) Irrationally, emotionally murderous.

c) Quite cross. But your mother was right: checkout chicks are rude as well as dumb.

3. You are going away for the weekend. Your destination is a three-hour drive away in your non-smoking car and you're not planning to stop on the way. How many times on this journey will you think about smoking?

a) Every five minutes.

b) Every 30 minutes or so.

c) Only twice – once after the first hour, then again about ten minutes or so from your destination.

4. The car gets stuck in traffic. Big traffic. You've hardly moved in the last ten minutes and the jam up ahead goes as far as the eye can see. *Now* **how many times do you think about smoking?**

a) Once – then you think: sod it! You wind down the window, light up, puff away furiously and, ignoring the driver's protests, extinguish your cigarette in the car's pristine ashtray.

b) Every five minutes.

c) A few times perhaps, but you can hang on until you get there – just about.

5. You finally reach your destination. You check into your hotel and head for the bar. It's non-smoking, but there's a pretty outdoor terrace where you can smoke. Once you have your drink/coffee/mineral water, where do you take it?

a) To a table outside – you like hurricanes. No really. They're bracing.

b) To a table outside – a few drops of rain never hurt anyone and it's bound to stop soon.

c) To a table outside – the sky is a beautiful, if slightly hazy blue, and 39°C isn't *that* hot.

How to score:
Mostly As: very dependent.
Mostly Bs: very dependent.
Mostly Cs: very dependent.

My absolute all-time favourite 'How addicted are you?' question found in a quit-smoking manual was 'Do you inhale?'

If you're an addicted smoker, the chances are that, given the opportunity, you'll smoke your greatest number of cigarettes early in the day and then gradually slow down as the day goes on. However, the waters have been well and truly muddied by the advent of large packs – a midwife friend has dubbed them mini-suitcases – containing 40 or even 50 cigarettes each with a negligible quantity of nicotine, like 1 mg. I asked my smokers to assess whether they were heavy, moderate, light or casual. More than half of those who regularly smoke anything from 20 to 45 cigarettes a day ticked 'moderate'. Surprised – because by anybody's standards I was a heavy smoker and I rarely smoked more than 30 a day on a bad day – I checked back through their questionnaires and found all were smoking cigarettes containing 4 mgs of nicotine or those almost nicotine-free 1-mg things. One poor woman who answered my survey is puffing up to 60 a day of these little blighters. She's not getting much nicotine but the mind boggles at the cocktail of chemicals her body is having to process from smoking that many cigarettes. I've got some advice for her – and those like her – in the next chapter.

Most experts agree that when you stop smoking you have two things to deal with: there's the chemical addiction to nicotine and the habit, the ritual side of smoking. If you are the kind of person who doesn't need to smoke soon after waking, does not feel anxious when you run out of cigarettes and can't get to the shops, does not need to light up in driving rain after a couple of hours in the cinema, and doesn't need to smoke when you're sick, your dependence on nicotine is probably more habitual than it is chemical. This does not necessarily mean you will find it easy to stop smoking but it does mean a shorter, less dramatic withdrawal period. In the next chapter we look at the various methods available – such as they are – to help smokers to quit.

Before I went into

analysis I told everyone

lies. But when you spend

all that money you start

to come clean.

JANE FONDA

10

Setting up a support system

THE METHOD YOU USE to stop smoking is not in itself the key to success or failure. All the standard ones – cold turkey, nicotine replacements, acupuncture, hypnotherapy – have the potential to succeed and fail in more or less equal proportions relative, of course, to their popularity. But whichever one you think might help you, there's no getting away from it – motivation is still a girl's best friend. If you wish with all your heart that you were not a smoker and if you think your life would be transformed if only you didn't need to smoke (which is true), then your chances of success are high however you choose to give up. Most of you know this from your previous efforts. But it's also true that taking advantage of the help that is available can give you an edge. Some smoking cessation therapy may be covered by your health fund. It's worth checking in advance . . . and if they say no, ask them why not?

Nicotine chewing gum is flavoured like a dirty ash-tray and gives you the hiccups – and you can't chew

gum and have a coffee or a beer. Hypnotherapy to me is a crock of s**t, rather like dealing with a used-car salesman while on Valium. Cold turkey has you passing smokers on the street and freaking out emotionally. *Sandi, 45, a smoker for 31 years, smokes 20–25 a day, once stopped for three months.*

cold turkey

Surveys suggest that simply throwing away your cigarettes, gritting your teeth and waiting for the withdrawal symptoms to pass is still the most common method of giving up smoking. It's a brave move that more than proves the mettle of those who succeed. Three-quarters of my ex-smokers gave up this way. But if you've gone cold turkey and only lasted a few weeks in the past, you can congratulate yourself. If you choose to do it this way again, next time could well be the winner.

how it works

Going cold turkey deprives your body of nicotine, the addictive substance in cigarettes, in one fell swoop. Since nicotine begins to leave the body almost as soon as you stub out a cigarette, if you can continue to ignore the cravings they eventually go away.

the bad news

When you go cold turkey you bear the full brunt of the withdrawal symptoms. These are covered fully in

Chapters 12 and 13, but they range from the initial cravings for a cigarette to irritability, appetite changes, lack of concentration, and mood swings.

the good news

If you can ride out the storm, you'll be over it more quickly than someone using nicotine replacement therapy (see below). Also, it won't cost you a cent. If you decide to go this route, it might be worth doing it in conjunction with a smoking cessation course (see page 96) in order to get that peer support. Or find yourself a quit buddy (see page 105).

Jumping straight to a nicotine-free life regardless of the consequences gave me a lot of strength and a sense of living in the future rather than the past. *Christine, 41, stopped cold turkey 18 months ago. A smoker for 17 years.*

I felt in control. It gets easier every time. *Ellen, 30, a smoker for 15 years. Stopped cold turkey two and a half months ago on her third attempt.*

nicotine replacement therapy

There is growing evidence that nicotine replacement therapy (NRT) currently available in the form of chewing gum or skin patches can help long-term heavy smokers to quit.

how it works

NRT supplies nicotine to your body, either through the mouth via the gum, or through the skin via a patch worn like a Band-Aid. NRT takes care of the chemical withdrawal, the physical craving for nicotine, leaving you free to deal with the psychological and habitual sides of smoking.

the bad news

When you stop the course of gum or patches, you'll experience some withdrawal symptoms. The manufacturers will probably deny this but they should listen to their customers. Although the cravings and other symptoms are much weaker than they would be when you jump straight from a pack of cigarettes a day to nothing, they still happen. And why wouldn't they? Like cigarettes, these products are putting nicotine into your system, so when you remove even the low dose supplied by the weakest patch or gum, your body is still going to react to some degree.

NRT is expensive. The recommended length of time for a course of patches is ten weeks. At the time of going to press prices start at around $30 for a seven-day supply of the strongest (21 mg) 24-hour patches; the 16-hour, 21-mg patches cost $25. The gum costs around $38 per pack of 105 pieces (heavy smokers may need to use up to ten pieces a day). Both are now available without prescription.

the good news

The gum helped me stop smoking for four months. It was the longest period I had gone without smoking cigarettes for 25 years, since childhood in fact. I agree with Sandi that the gum doesn't taste fantastic, and you have to take care not to over-chew the stuff or you get the sensation of having pure nicotine going down your throat. Yuk! And, of course, Sandi is right when she observes that you can't enjoy a beer or a coffee – those traditional bosom buddies of cigarettes – with a piece of gum in your mouth. But I'm not sure that's such a bad thing when you are trying to break the association!

Two years later and extremely motivated (see Chapter 11), I opted for the patches – and they were brilliant. And I assure you, the manufacturers have not paid me a cent to say this . . . more's the pity because I'm definitely one of their success stories! Like the gum, the patches took care of the cravings and helped me put some distance between my last cigarette and my new life as a non-smoker. Unlike the gum, they were invisible, hidden neatly under clothing on various parts of the body. And while I had no problem with the most commonly reported side-effect of the 24-hour patches – those vivid, busy dreams – for those who do, the 16-hour patches, which you remove before going to bed, should fix it.

quit-smoking courses

Only a small percentage of the ex-smokers who
responded to my survey used one of these courses, with
just one ex-smoker reporting that she quit successfully
by using a combination of cold turkey and a very
expensive private quit course. The rest gave them a miss
and my smokers, meanwhile, felt strongly that they
shouldn't have to pay through the nose to give up. I
couldn't agree more. However, the ex-smoker who
forked out all that money was not complaining – she
was ecstatic to be free of nicotine, so for her it was
money well spent.

how they work

You get individual or group counselling to help you
overcome the need for cigarettes and nicotine. I'd recommend such a course if you're planning to go cold
turkey. These courses may also provide some additional
armoury for those using nicotine replacement therapy.
If you like the idea of a course, call the national Quit
line (131 848 Australia-wide) for details of your nearest group or class. If you live in or around a city, you are
likely to be offered a bewildering array of courses,
which range from expensive private ones ($360 for
seven weeks) to a charitable $50 for eight sessions over
four weeks, right down to free one-to-one counselling
offered by a sympathetic social worker from your local
women's health centre.

the bad news

Before you pay up, make sure the course coordinator is qualified to help you. I signed up for an evening course at my local hospital, which was quite reasonably priced at $60 for six weeks. On the first night of the course, with the help of nicotine gum, I hadn't smoked for 11 days – my then personal best – so I was feeling quite pleased with myself. My fellow course-mates, however, had all gone cold turkey the previous day or that same day and were feeling pretty agitated and unhappy.

The course coordinator was a government health department employee who was moonlighting to earn some extra cash. I have no problem with that. But this was clearly not her forte. I don't know what her quali- fications were for running the group but what I remember is that she had been put in charge of 12 very stressed-out men and women and she hadn't a clue what was going on. One brave soul spoke out and one by one we all gave her our first-hand experiences of nicotine withdrawal. Despite her claim to have once been a smoker, some 20-odd years before, she was astonished. There was nothing in her experience or her instruction manual to prepare her for this. Which left us counselling one another during coffee breaks. The con- sensus was that the course was a waste of money.

the good news

A few things have changed since I gave up smoking. For a start, when (just prior to publication) I rang the national Quit line posing as a smoker looking to stop, the person who answered the phone couldn't have been more pleasant or helpful (which was not my experience when I was quitting for real and in the throes of withdrawal!). That phone number, 131 848, is shared by all the government-funded Quit organisations in each Australian state so the level of service offered will vary depending on where you live. But the line is open 24 hours a day, seven days a week and for the cost of a local call offers practical information on quitting, telephone counselling, and even an interpreter service.

I don't think you can have too much help when you're giving up smoking. However, to ensure you get the right kind of help, investigate all your options – preferably before you smoke your last cigarette – and don't be afraid to ask questions. It might help to write them all down before you pick up the phone rather than trying to think on your feet. If I was looking to stop smoking now with the help of a course, I'd want to know what I'd be getting for my money: what the course program involves, what the counsellor's qualifications are (being a recent ex-smoker would be a definite plus for me) and what ongoing support is available once the course has ended.

hypnotherapy

Hypnosis is the process by which a person induces 'an altered state of awareness' in another person by putting you in a state of deep relaxation. Once in that state, the practitioner can then induce you to change undesired behaviour patterns, like smoking.

how it works

Once you are in that state of deep relaxation, hypnosis is said to work in this case by planting an aversion to smoking in your subconscious. This is done over a number of sessions, around five to ten. But since anyone can call themselves a hypnotherapist and take out an advertisement in the local paper, you'll need to take care. A personal recommendation from a satisfied client is always good. Otherwise contact the Australian Society of Hypnosis in your state for the names of your nearest registered practitioners, who should be either a psychologist or a medical practitioner. (You can find the address in the White Pages, or contact the Federal office in Victoria: phone (03) 9429 8240; or email hypnosis@alphalink.com.au) Costs vary, but start at around $80 per session.

the bad news

It didn't work for me. I was hypnotised one day in my lunch break and smoked a cigarette in the taxi on the way back to work less than an hour later. But I was a non-believer to begin with. If you think this might work for you, then it might.

the good news

I've known two big smokers who used hypnotherapy to quit smoking successfully; one very level-headed woman, a die-hard 40-a-day (12 mg) addict; and one 50-a-day male smoker with a degree in cynicism. The woman stopped smoking for three years after hypnotherapy and her subsequent lapse back into smoking was clearly not due to the failure of the hypnosis! She's now getting ready to quit again and plans to use the same method. As for my cynical male ex-colleague, the last I heard he was still a non-smoker after 15 years.

acupuncture

This is an ancient Chinese medical practice which involves inserting tiny needles into 'pressure' points in the body. It is a holistic approach that uses the principle of mind and body working together to combat disease. Another alternative quit-smoking therapy which, if you already accept its merits, could be the answer to your prayers.

how it works

Acupuncture is said to promote detoxification and help relieve the withdrawal symptoms, both physical and emotional, through a series of treatments over four weeks or so. To find a registered practitioner in your area, use that great information source known as word of mouth, or contact the Australian Acupuncture &

Chinese Medicine Association on its national toll-free number: 1800 025 334. Expect to pay around $50 per session.

the bad news

I don't know one person who has given up smoking for longer than a few days using this method.

the good news

I once saw a television documentary in which a man was having a heart and lung transplant with acupuncture as the only means of anaesthetic. He was wide awake while they were cutting him open and these needles were the only things that were stopping him feeling the pain of the surgeon's knife. If this practice can block the pain of major surgery I don't have any problem believing it might be able to do the same for nicotine withdrawal symptoms. If it works for you, let me know!

aversion therapy

This is where you force yourself to smoke at least half a dozen cigarettes one after the other and then feel so ill you don't ever want to touch the things again. My friend's dad held her down and forced her to smoke a large cigar after finding a packet of cigarettes in her school bag when she was 12. It did put her off smoking cigarettes, as it happened . . . but it put her off her dad too. These days, she could probably sue him.

If this form of nicotine cessation therapy is still prac-
tised anywhere in Australia those doing it are keeping it
very quiet. I can see how it might work on a child
(although I wouldn't use it on mine!) but if the morning
after a party – and the revolting feeling in your mouth,
throat and lungs, the smell in your clothes and hair, the
sight of those overflowing ashtrays – isn't enough to put
an adult off smoking, neither will this kind of horror show.

cutting down

This one works on the logic that if you cut down the
number of cigarettes you smoke each day, eventually
you'll find it easier to give up. We've all tried this at
some point in our smoking lives. But while our bodies
no doubt benefit from each cigarette we don't smoke,
cutting down is not a precursor to giving up. It just
gives us a false sense of security. 'If I can cut down from
20 a day to 10 a day it means I've got my smoking
under control and I'll eventually be able to give up.' No
it doesn't, really. It means that by giving your willpower
a workout you can reduce the amount you smoke for
a limited period of time – a day or two, a week or two,
a month or two even – until your next big night out, or
the next major stress attack. The result of this well-
intentioned deprivation is that when you do allow
yourself to smoke, it feels wonderful. Rationing yourself to only those cigarettes that make you feel good is
not a great motivator for giving up.

changing brands

This one works on the principle that switching from your favourite brand of cigarettes to one you don't like, or one containing a lower amount of nicotine, can lead you towards eventually giving up. Lots of people do this – every second smoker I see these days is carrying low-nicotine cigarettes. Non-smokers, of course, will be amazed to hear that any cigarette could taste anything other than revolting but the connoisseurs among us know differently. Some brands are very smooth and some are not. If you have the willpower to switch from a smooth brand to a foul-tasting brand and smoke them for longer than a day or two, trust me when I tell you that you have the willpower to give up completely. So don't pay good money for old rope. Stick with your favourite brand, then set yourself a quit date.

Similarly, if you switched from your favourite brand to a low-nicotine brand, the chances are you now smoke far more cigarettes than you did before. That's because your body needs a certain amount of nicotine every day, come what may, and in order to get it from those nasty little 1-mg things, you practically need to chain-smoke. Bearing in mind that the most hazardous component of a cigarette is not the nicotine at all but the attendant cocktail of chemicals, you are better off getting more nicotine from fewer cigarettes. So if you've been struggling along on these paper excuses and seen your consumption go up, switch back to your favourite brand and watch the number of cigarettes you smoke plummet. Only then should you think about giving up. Because when you stop smoking the first withdrawal symptoms to go are the physical cravings for nicotine. More persistent are the psychological withdrawal symptoms: some call it a grieving process over the loss of an undesirable but irresistible friend. I reckon coming to terms with the loss of a 15–20-a-day bad friend must be easier than coping with the loss of a 60-a-day friend.

new developments

For this ex-smoker, the most interesting new development is the use of drugs which are designed to work on serotonin and dopamine, the 'happy hormones' in the brain. These are not yet available to smokers in Australia although one, Zyban, is currently being trialled and received some Viagra-style pre-publicity in October 1999 that should have prompted a stampede! Licensed in the US as a smoking cessation aid, Zyban is said to prevent cravings for both nicotine and chocolate, help you lose weight and cause spontaneous multiple orgasms. I want it and I want it now!

The latest addition to the NRT range in Australia is the Inhaler, from Nicorette. Resembling a plastic cigarette, only without the chemicals, the nicotine is supplied via cartridges fitted to a mouthpiece. Available from pharmacies without prescription, at $39.95 for a week's supply.

find a friend

Whichever method you choose your chances of success increase immeasurably the more support you have. A non-smoking partner, or an equally well-motivated smoking partner who is prepared to give up with you, would be top of my list. My partner and I gave up together and I'm sure that contributed to my eventual success and possibly to my partner's success too.

Alternatively, or even in addition, tell a close friend or relative you are going to stop smoking and ask if they mind you phoning them from time to time if the going gets tough. Anyone who cares about you is better than nobody at all, but obviously the most qualified person to help you through those difficult early days is someone who knows first-hand what you're going through – i.e. someone who has given up smoking themselves and come out the other end smiling.

> **I gave up with two other people. I lived next door to one of them. We talked it through constantly. It was good having people around who knew exactly what you were going through.** *Ann, 35, a smoker for 17 years. Hasn't smoked for 22 months. Went cold turkey.*

Don't be afraid to look outside your immediate circle. I received some casual but invaluable support from an ex-colleague. Our lives were very different but she'd given up smoking a year before me and knew exactly what I was going through. The empathy and understanding she

could pack into a two-minute conversation was enough
to send me happily on my way for another few days.

If you have access to a public noticeboard, either at
work or in your community (public library, community
centre, coffee shop, supermarket), you could even
advertise for a support person. I'm serious. When I was
first at home in a new suburb with a new baby after 21
years in the workforce, I wrote the following advertisement: 'Mother on maternity leave with three-month-old
baby going stir crazy. Would anyone in a similar situation like to get together in the daytime for coffee, chats,
laughs, etc.?' In the first week I received calls from three
women who lived locally whose babies were around the
same age as mine. Four years later we are still friends,
as are our now strapping offspring. There were others
who responded to that advertisement who came and
went. But we all gained something from knowing one
another, even for a short time.

The ability to talk easily on a personal level with
complete strangers is a talent most women have, and it's
one that can be used to very good advantage in this
instance. Give it a try. It won't cost you anything and
you have nothing to lose but your nicotine addiction!

I might repeat to myself

slowly and soothingly,

a list of quotations

beautiful from minds

profound . . . if I can

remember any of the

damn things.

DOROTHY PARKER

11

Countdown
to Q-day

OKAY! YOU ARE MEGA-MOTIVATED, you've been sending those 840 rogue kilojoules on their way each day for at least three weeks and you've sorted out your method of giving up. So when is the happy day?

As I said in Chapter 8, spring is a time of new life and also a good time spiritually to start *your* new life as a non-smoker. But, really, any time of year is a good time to stop smoking. What matters is that you are ready for action and that your confidence in your ability to stop is at its peak.

all in the timing

Well, almost any time is good . . . try to pick a moment when life is relatively unstressful. I know this is difficult: we all lead very busy lives, with many of us chasing our tails a lot of the time. But some periods are likely to be less frantic than others and therefore more conducive to giving up smoking successfully. Life events which send the anxiety levels racing off the Richter Scale are the big five: marriage, divorce or separation, moving house, changing jobs and bereavement. So try to delay giving up smoking if any of those are looming – not that you can plan things like bereavement.

Which is a point worth remembering. Life will hit you with whatever it has in store whether you smoke cigarettes or not. And it's also worth keeping in mind that the relief we get from a stressful situation when we inhale a cigarette and the smoke hits that spot in the back of the throat is only fleeting. Plus, as we know only too well, being a smoker is stressful in its own right. Not smoking will, ultimately, reduce your overall stress levels.

What can also dictate the time you choose to stop smoking is a specific life event, something happening that makes the timing perfect. For me it was two things: I was three and a half months away from a 26-hour flight between Sydney and London and back again. With a toddler. And the only airlines I consider safe enough to transport me and mine were non-smoking, as most airlines are now. Sydney airport was by now a non-smoking airport, and I'd heard rumours that London's Heathrow was heading that way . . . not that it mattered. I knew I wouldn't make it beyond the economy-class baggage check-in at Sydney airport without a cigarette. As well as being a nicotine addict, I'm a nervous flier too.

So just as I was wondering how to go about organising a general anaesthetic to last me from Sydney to

London, along came incentive number two – surgery to replace my two front teeth, which had been knocked out when I was mugged 17 years previously. My original teeth were successfully replanted the night of the mugging, but they were always on borrowed time. So when they became too wobbly for words, I opted for implants. This permanent but expensive (and painful) solution is done in several stages, each dependent on the other. The first was to take place after my trip to England.

My long-time dentist, who I'd trust with my life and who never hassled me about my smoking (or my wobbly front teeth), casually suggested that I might think about giving up smoking before the first stage of the surgery in order to maximise the chances of its success. He explained that because smoking constricts the blood flow around the body, it retards the healing process. So I could go through all the pain and expense and blow it all ('scuse the pun) by smoking. That did it. The next day I got a two-week supply of patches and gave myself seven days' notice to quit.

Three months later, I arrived in London a new person. My family and friends couldn't believe it. Neither could I. Rediscovering life without my 27-year addiction was unreal. One of the best parts was going to non-smoking places and losing track of the time. It doesn't sound like much, but previously I would have been twitching for a cigarette after an hour or so, to the point where all pleasure and enjoyment would end and the need for nicotine would override everything. Smokers never lose track of the time unless they are free to smoke! This was wonderful.

My subsequent surgery was a success too. And when one area seemed to be taking its time to heal, I rang my dentist and had a whinge with a clear conscience. As a smoker, I always tried to suffer pain and discomfort in silence because I never wanted to hear those judgemental words 'Well, if you didn't smoke . . .'

do drink and be merry, but . . .

When you're setting the big date, it's also helpful to aim for a gap in your life that is free of major social events – Christmas, New Year, other high days and holidays, family celebrations, best friend's wedding, overseas trips, big nights out – anything where you might be tempted to smoke, especially if you're a drinker. I regard much of the prevailing advice on giving up smoking instantly rejectable, but one recurring message that makes sense to me *with the benefit of hindsight* is the one about avoiding alcohol for the first few weeks after giving up.

I didn't, and for me having a glass or two of wine with dinner – which I would do anyway – helped fill that void of not smoking. But there's no doubt that it also sometimes triggered the urge to smoke. At home, or in any other smoke-free environment, the cravings passed quickly and painlessly. However, with a drink in my hand and a smoker nearby – especially one smoking my old brand – I found things a little uncomfortable. Even after two years, I still get twinges. Which won't surprise the ex-smokers who responded to my survey, since more than half admitted they still occasionally get the urge to smoke. In what circumstances? The combination of alcohol and being around smokers were top of the list of triggers.

Of course, curtailing your social life is no problem when you are a parent. What social life? I hear mothers cry. Exactly. But if you're footloose and seriously social, now is the time for some lateral thinking. First, for the reasons given above, plan to give your smoking friends a wide berth for those first few critical weeks. I know you don't want to hear this. You don't want to be the kind of ex-smoker who makes her smoking friends feel bad. But if they are real friends, they won't take it personally and they'll still be there when you feel strong enough to be around them without being tempted to smoke yourself.

Next, organise a night out with some non-smokers. What do you mean, you don't know any? Of course you do. And even though we know you've been avoiding us lately, we'd love to have a night out with you. Most of us are good fun to be around when we're not getting cigarette smoke blown in our faces. Many of us are ex-smokers too, and we know exactly where you're at. So you get to have an enjoyable, safe night out, with some moral support thrown in. What are you waiting for?

Soon you will discover what I, and ex-smokers everywhere, have discovered . . . that it's brilliant being a non-smoker. And I know that, deep down, you wish you didn't have to go through this. You'd like to wake up tomorrow and read a newspaper headline that said something like 'Smokers Live Longer – It's Official!' or 'A Cigarette a Day Keeps the Doctor Away' or 'Sir Walter Raleigh Was a Genius' or 'Government Says Sorry to Smokers' (I like the sound of the last one!), but you know that smoking is uncool, unattractive, smelly, unhealthy, overpriced and, like my wobbly two front teeth, on borrowed time.

Those of you who have reached this point before probably wish you didn't have to read the next couple of chapters. Believe me, I'm right there with you because I know that tomorrow and the next few weeks are not going to be easy. You are going to be withdrawing from one of the most addictive substances on the planet, and doing so while having to go to work, care for the kids, cook dinner and go to the supermarket. It's a very tall order . . .

But aim to take one day at a time. Survive the first ten days and know that the worst is well and truly over. Hold on for another ten, and your emotions may still be a bit topsy-turvy but you will have moments of pure exhilaration. Your body, meanwhile, will love you to pieces. You will be able to breathe more easily, your tastebuds will tingle, your breath will smell nice, your hair will smell nice, your clothes will smell nice, and you'll have noticeably more energy. Oh, and by the way, you'll be free! Here are some thoughts to take with you into the next chapter and beyond, and to help spur you on into this new and wonderful phase in your life:

1. Giving up smoking will put you back in control of your life. Smoking removes that control.

2. If you think you can do it, you can do it. If you think you can't, you're right.

3. When you feel anxious, you want to smoke. Yet the relief you get from smoking a cigarette is so temporary. Anyway, being a smoker makes you feel anxious.

4. Giving up smoking will remove a major cause of stress and anxiety from your life.

5. Giving up smoking will leave you free to deal better with the everyday stresses in your life that you can't remove.

6. As a recreational drug, nicotine has had its day.

7. Give up smoking and live long enough to get back some of your tobacco taxes.

8. Give up smoking and live long enough to be a nuisance to your children.

9. Give up smoking and enjoy the sensation of annoying the hell out of the government. Deep in their avaricious hearts, they don't want you to give up smoking. They need the money. I say don't give them another cent!

10. Giving up smoking will send your self-esteem soaring.

Modern drugs are wonderful. They enable a wife with pneumonia to nurse her husband through flu.

JILLY COOPER

12

From Q-day to day ten

YOUR FIRST TEN DAYS as a non-smoker are likely to be among the hardest and, surprisingly, the easiest days to get through. On the one hand, the physical symptoms of withdrawal are at their most acute, but on the other, you are feeling full of resolve and, let's face it, pretty excited. There is a huge novelty value in waking up each day and experiencing life very differently from the way you've been living it up to now. For some of you, it may be the first time you've experienced adult life without cigarettes. That was true for me and I felt like I'd been reborn.

But for me it is the little things that leave the strongest impression. The space in my bag that used to contain my cigarettes (usually two packs – I was always terrified of running out) and lighters. The spare time in the mornings now that I no longer needed to smoke three or four cigarettes before leaving the house. The first meal in a restaurant when I actually ate the food I'd ordered instead of nibbling at it half-heartedly and all the time wanting the meal to end so I could smoke.

Feeling a part of the human race instead of apart from it. As someone who has been swimming against the tide for much of my life, going with the flow for once makes a nice change. Fleur, 38, a smoker for 25 years, puts it this way: 'I can go anywhere I like without feeling like a social leper.'

Using the patches helped me a lot. They took the edge off the physical withdrawal symptoms while allowing me to revel in some of the immediate benefits of giving up – being able to breathe more easily, smelling sweeter, having more energy, plus all the senses being heightened. Not to mention ending each day with the knowledge that I'd put another day's distance between myself and my last cigarette.

In this chapter you'll find some of the responses to the question 'What's the best thing about giving up smoking?' Some others include 'Not coughing in the mornings', 'Being able to rely on myself and not a drug', 'Being able to enjoy social gatherings without the anxiety of needing to smoke', 'Being able to taste food properly for the first time in years' and so on. These are just some of the things you have to look forward to in the coming weeks and months.

> **I smell better and I no longer have the fear that I won't be able to have a smoke when I want one – like on a plane overseas.** *Catherine, 41, a smoker for 26 years, smoked 15–20 a day. Hasn't smoked for five months.*

My house smells lovely. My clothes don't smell. I can run on the treadmill for ten minutes at a time. *Sophie, 27, a smoker for eight years, smoked 35 a day. Hasn't smoked for 29 days.*

Feeling so much better. In the beginning I was terrified of putting on weight, like I had when I'd tried to stop in the past. So, reluctantly, I started going to the gym – I found one that offered free childcare. And to my amazement I loved it. Now I'm training for a half marathon. My friends all joke I've turned into a gym junkie, but I don't care. I've quit smoking and I feel fantastic. *Lyn, 37, a smoker for 22 years, smoked 25 a day. Hasn't smoked for three months.*

Whether you're using nicotine replacement therapy or not, you're going to need to find some creative ways to deal with the withdrawal symptoms. I look at these in detail in the next chapter. But for the first ten days, the strongest symptoms are likely to be the burning need for nicotine, the desire to cram everything and anything into your mouth, and the sometimes overwhelming feelings of agitation. Following is a selection of everyday diversions which should help when any one of these feelings hits. Try to keep in mind that every day you don't smoke will weaken these feelings until one day, very soon, you will wake up and they will be gone.

Half the time, what you'll miss as much as actually smoking is the ritual of smoking. As one who took smoke breaks on the footpath outside the office, for a while after quitting I missed the camaraderie, but I especially missed the gossip. All the best office stories used to break on that footpath. I got over it, though. And some of my fellow smokers joined me as non-smokers. What none of us missed about those pavement gatherings was the pitying/disdainful looks we used to get from passers-by.

crave crushers

The need for oral gratification, in particular sugar, is big in the first days. So keep that lolly jar handy and filled up during this time. Pretend you're a kid again and rediscover all those teeth-shattering goodies you used to enjoy. Only this time around you can dip into it whenever you feel the urge and you don't even have to share. It's my personal favourite because it really does the job. If you are really concerned about kilojoules, go for the old favourite: a water cracker with a dob of low-kilojoule jam. Or you could even try Neil Grunberg's no-joule suggestion of sprinkling a sugar substitute like Nutrasweet on anything healthy that comes to hand – a stick of celery, a piece of apple, a water cracker, whatever.

listen to your body

Your body might even ask for some of those healthy things that the other quit-smoking guides tell you to keep handy to fight cravings. Like raw carrot and celery sticks without sugar substitute, or fresh fruit or low-kilojoule snacks. But if it doesn't and you want to eat a family-sized bag of potato chips or a block of chocolate in one sitting, do it. Your body is going through a major chemical change. Listen to what it's telling you and do what you have to do to get past the next ten days without smoking. This is only a short-term measure.

driven to distraction?

Get up and walk around. If you're at work, go to the toilet, read a noticeboard, start a conversation with somebody, take a message to another department. Collect some supplies, or order some. If you're not too busy, phone somebody up. Stuff it: even if you are busy, phone someone up. Preferably one of your support people, or someone you know who can always make you laugh. Most of us work too hard these days anyway, and I'm sure your manager will want to be seen to be supporting your efforts to make yourself more productive by no longer needing to take smokos!

If none of this is practical, mentally plan yourself a treat. Or take some deep breaths and say to yourself, 'I don't smoke.' And revel in being able to say that. If you can find a way to distract yourself, the craving will pass quickly. With smoking so restricted in most workplaces, you probably won't find too much temptation in your path in working hours. Dangerous moments will be those when you would normally take a break for a cigarette – morning tea, lunch, mid-afternoon. Use any means available to you to vary your routine and do something else at those times. Also try to pick a moment when you feel okay (and there will be some!) to think about what you're going to do when the next craving or attack of agitation hits. That will be easier than trying to think rationally when you feel like you've got rats gnawing away inside you.

home comforts

At home, there are myriad possible distractions. Just getting up and doing something, anything, that you couldn't do with a cigarette in your hand can see off a craving. So can brushing your teeth, or drinking a glass of water or a glass of fruit juice. For some reason, I found a glass of orange juice could ease a craving (probably because of the sugar). As a smoker I rarely drank it, finding it too acidic. But I drank litres of it when I stopped smoking. Go figure!

aversion therapy!

One quit book suggests keeping a screw-top jar full of butts and taking a sniff to ward off a craving. I like that one. I only came across it after I quit, otherwise I would definitely have tried it. The smell from a freshly lit cigarette is one thing, but sticking your nose into the equivalent of an unemptied ashtray would dispel fairly quickly any romantic notions you may be harbouring.

reap the rewards

Avoid making long-term or life-altering plans and decisions until you've been off the fags for at least three months, or until you feel 'normal' again, whichever is the sooner. Meanwhile, though, plan some well-deserved treats for yourself. If you're using nicotine replacement therapy, your cigarette money is spoken for just now, but you can banish a craving just by thinking of some of the good things to spend it on when it's freed up – which will be in just a few weeks. This advice comes to you with the benefit of hindsight. At the time of quitting, a pack of my old brand cost $7-plus (depending on where I bought them); at a pack a day, that's around $50 a week or $200 a month or $2600 per year. Unfortunately, my year's worth of cigarette money was all spoken for in advance with my trip to the UK, plus my dental surgery. Since I'm not the world's greatest saver, I suppose my reward was the $2600 that didn't end up on my credit card that year!

I worked with a man who, when he stopped smoking, saved up his cigarette money and bought himself a bicycle. Another reckons he put his 'under the mattress' until he had enough saved for a term deposit at the bank. An informal straw poll among the women I know, however, produced no such stories. Instead, they reported things like buying a few new clothes or some make-up, having a night out, getting a weekly massage for a few weeks, having lunch out with a girlfriend. These are all nice treats but they are only short-term. After that, the money just seems to get absorbed into the household coffers. I say if you've been spending money on cigarettes for 20 years and suddenly you stop smoking, that money saved is YOURS to be used for YOURSELF to benefit YOU in the long term.

With interest rates so low, it isn't easy to get a good return on your money in regular bank accounts. But there are other ways you can invest $50 a week FOR YOURSELF. Am I over-emphasising the FOR YOURSELF bit? Yes? Good. A boring but sensible move would be to divert it to your Super or your home loan. Risky but more fun would be a dabble in stocks and shares. The share-market, for instance, is becoming an option for regular folk these days. The floating of public companies such as Telstra has opened the door to what the financial wizards are calling the mum and dad investors. They mean some of us. Then there are things like investment clubs, which allow people with only small amounts of cash to spare to pool resources and potentially make lots of money, and have some fun at the same time. Better late than never, that's what I now plan to do with that $50 a week I'm not spending on cigarettes.

cheap and cheerful

Enjoyable treats and distractions that don't cost much
are a bit thin on the ground, but they are out there if
you're motivated to look. It depends on what you're
into and what's available in your area, but generally aim
for pursuits or places where you couldn't smoke even if
you wanted to, like the cinema (go on half-price day),
art gallery, public library or the museum. If you haven't
been to a museum since schooldays, go and check one
out. They have been transformed from the mind-
numbingly boring, hands-off kind of places that I
remember from school visits to interesting, high-tech,
button-pressing centres of learning and fun.

read all about it!

Another absorbing way to kill some smoke-free time is
in a bookstore. You don't have to spend a cent. But for
the price of a pack or three of cigarettes you could buy
the latest best-seller . . . or one of the several user-
friendly investment advice books. There are even a
couple written *by* women *for* women.

indulge yourself

If you like having your body pampered, book a massage,
a manicure, a facial – whatever turns you on. And don't
forget to tell the beautician you've given up smoking. In
fact, don't miss any opportunity to mention to someone

that you've given up smoking. It helps pass the time and may see off a craving; and, as you are probably thinking constantly about smoking anyway, airing some of those thoughts can be very therapeutic. Some of them might even be ex-smokers and have a few good tips for you!

Go to the dentist and get your teeth cleaned and polished. I did this. It's a great motivator not to smoke. In fact, failure though I was at giving up smoking all those years, each time I walked out of the dentist with beautifully cleaned and polished teeth, I used to think seriously about tossing my cigarettes in the nearest bin and giving up anything else that was likely to take the shine off them. Like food, for instance!

spring into action!

Get your clothes, curtains, carpets and upholstery cleaned to get rid of the smell of smoke. And take advantage of the excess energy you may be experiencing to do some spring cleaning. For instance, if you start washing down the paintwork with sugar soap, you will be rewarded by the sight of layers of tar dissolving in the bucket and the true colours of your decor sparkling away at you. And you can toss out all your ashtrays and the out-of-gas $2 lighters that you'll find around the house in all sorts of hidden places, like behind cupboards, under cushions, in rarely used handbags.

pat yourself on the back

Look at people who are smoking and instead of envying them, be glad it's not you. One day, they are going to have to do what you've just done: give up smoking. I bet they envy you. And why wouldn't they? You're one of life's achievers. Just to remind you, here again is what you've achieved by becoming a non-smoker:

- Reduced your chances of developing lung cancer, emphysema, chronic bronchitis, heart disease, stroke, gangrene. Within two to five years of quitting your risk of getting any of these life-threatening conditions is reduced by half and after ten years, your risk is the same as that of someone who has never smoked.

- Made it safer to take the contraceptive pill, particularly if you are over 30. The medics reckon women who smoke and take the pill are 19 times more likely to die of a heart attack or stroke than a woman who doesn't smoke, and the over 30s are most at risk.

- Improved your fertility and turned back your body clock. Women who smoke seem to go through the menopause some two or three years earlier than women who don't.

- Made guilt-free pregnancy and breast-feeding a reality. Ditto guilt-free parenting. Now if your child is unfortunate enough to suffer from asthma or any recurring respiratory infections, those who like to play the blame game will have to look elsewhere for a reason.

- Improved the blood flow around your body making your skin look pinker, healthier and younger. In particular, you'll retard the development of those fine vertical lines above your mouth that are oh-so-ageing. Some of us regret not stopping before they developed!
- Boosted your self-confidence. If you can quit smoking, you can do anything!

I asked my husband to restore my confidence. I told him my boobs were gone, my stomach was gone. I asked him to say something nice about my legs. 'Blue goes with everything,' he said.

JOAN RIVERS

13

Chain reaction

Today I woke up angry. I knew it was going to be a bad day. I shouted at my partner for forgetting to refill the filtered water jug the night before. Said it was symptomatic of a lack of feeling for me. Yelled at my child for taking too long to get dressed. Then felt guilty. Went for a brisk walk hoping some happy hormones would kick in. Instead, had homicidal thoughts towards the owner of a car parked across a driveway that I had to walk into the road to get round. Ditto the owner of a Rottweiler who by allowing his/her beast to take itself for a walk, caused me a half-mile detour to avoid it. I am terrified of large, unleashed, unaccompanied dogs. Happy hormones wouldn't come. Had murderous thoughts about fierce dogs and their owners all the way home. Dubbed them slavering penis extensions. The dogs, I mean. Later in the day discovered some wages I was expecting to find in the bank weren't there, due to an administrative cock-up. Was calm to begin with and then it started to fester and I seethed all day.

> **Finally, I left my work bag on the bus and had hys-
> terics at the bus company.** *From* Diary of a Mad
> Woman, *a smoker for 27 years, smoked 25 a day, hasn't
> smoked for two years. Felt 'human' again after 12 weeks
> without smoking, and not bad at all after 16 weeks.*

WHEN I SAT DOWN to write this chapter I suddenly
understood why, in their enthusiasm to get you to stop
smoking, so many of the other quit guides gloss over
the withdrawal symptoms. Deep down, bless them, they
care about you. So much so that they can't bring themselves to admit that you are going to feel like shite for
the next few weeks and perhaps even several months –
and that there's not a great deal you can do about it
except to hang in there and wait for it all to pass.

I wish I didn't have to write this chapter. I'd like to
be able to offer you nothing but positive, happy thoughts.
But most people who quit smoking will experience some
or all of the following withdrawal symptoms to a greater
or lesser degree. I don't see how it helps anybody to pretend otherwise.

The good news is that while all the major withdrawal symptoms – cravings, irritability, lack of
concentration, mood swings – were experienced by the
vast majority of my ex-smokers, by far the most trou-
blesome and long-lasting symptom was weight gain.
And that's one problem you don't have to face. You
should already have it licked. (If you haven't, Chapter
16 is just for you.) But what you do have to face is that

you have just removed from your body an addictive substance it has become used to, fond of even, over the years and in so doing you have sent it into a flat spin. Soon – much sooner than you think – your body will love you forever. But until then it needs time to adjust to its new lifestyle.

increased energy

Let's start with a good one. Increased energy is a positive, happy and almost immediate side-effect of quitting smoking that gripped about half my ex-smokers. I experienced it too, and after more than two years I am happy to report I still have it. Do with it what you will, but be sure to enjoy it.

nicotine cravings

Since nicotine begins to leave your body almost before you've extinguished your last cigarette, the cravings are the first withdrawal symptom to hit you. They are also the first to disappear. The burning, chemical need for nicotine will be felt particularly by those of you who have gone cold turkey. The urges will periodically descend on you in waves and will be most acute during the first three to five days. After that they begin to taper off. Within ten days or so they should disappear almost without you noticing, probably because your attention has been well and truly diverted by the burning need to murder somebody. (See Irritability, below.) Some of the diversionary tactics suggested in the previous chapter should help see the cravings off.

The need for oral gratification is at its height while you have cravings. As I said in the last chapter, do what you have to do to avoid smoking. If you find you're still getting the urge to cram everything and anything into your mouth after about ten days, get your fat counter out and make sure what you are putting in won't easily convert to body fat. Although avoiding cigarettes is your main priority right now, you don't want to sabotage the weight control measures you put in place before quitting.

withdrawal pangs

Hard to describe, but different from cravings. I experienced them as an empty, gnawing feeling deep in the pit of my being, a description which struck a chord with more than half my respondents who ticked yes to this one. For me, these pangs seemed to take over where the cravings left off, and while the gnawing feeling disappeared within a few weeks, I find I still get the 'empty' feeling occasionally and very fleetingly. But I was a smoker for 27 years.

irritability

Like cravings and withdrawal pangs, this was another big one that affected more than three-quarters of my ex-smokers. My questionnaire asked them to list the order in which the withdrawal symptoms disappeared, and irritability was frequently put third behind cravings and withdrawal pangs. Which will be a relief to those of you who are getting the urge to choke the living daylights out of almost everyone you meet. Take lots of deep breaths, do lots of counting to ten, use any diversionary tactic you can think of, and try to keep in mind that you are in the process of withdrawing from one of the most addictive drugs on the planet. It's no wonder you feel cranky. But, honestly, the people you are forced to mix with are being no more irritating than usual and, even if they are, you can't murder them. Smoking is endemic in prison.

vagueness, light-headedness, dizziness

Just over one-third of my ex-smokers ticked yes to these three, any one of which could be due to the increased oxygen that is now flowing around your body. Or it could be the low blood-sugar levels that cause your body to crave sugar or carbohydrates – another excuse to reach for the jelly-bean jar, or to have a yummy bowl of pasta. These symptoms do not usually become a problem, and they should disappear fairly quickly.

anxiety, restlessness

Less than a quarter of my ex-smokers ticked yes for these two, but I remember them well, especially the feelings of restlessness and insecurity which would hit me in waves, some of them quite powerful, from time to time during the early days. Another similar description from one of my respondents that struck a chord with me was *a sense of vulnerability*. I recall that feeling too. Of those women who ticked yes for these symptoms, about half found them difficult to overcome.

The distractions suggested in Chapter 12 should help. Or if you are finding these feelings a real problem, you could see your doctor about getting an anti-depressant or mild tranquilliser to take for a week or two. I had some 5-mg diazepam left over from a plane trip (I told you I was a nervous flier!) and in order to keep my world ticking over during this tricky period, I broke them in half and popped half a tab from time to time as needed. I took them for about three weeks, or until they ran out – I can't remember which came first. This paragraph caused great alarm to one GP who read my manuscript. 'Beware of swapping one addiction with another,' she cautioned. I considered that fair comment, which is why I am sharing it with you. But by the same token, I was dismayed at the implication that women who are addicted to nicotine are somehow predisposed to any old addiction. It's worth noting that I haven't come across one person who has given up cigarettes and become addicted to tranquillisers! However, I'm not recommending self-medication, so do talk to your doctor if these symptoms become too difficult.

If you don't want to resort to prescription drugs, there are natural/homoeopathic remedies available that have a calming effect. Chamomile, valerian, Bach Flower Remedy are just three that can be found on the shelves of most supermarkets or health food stores. If you are interested in relaxation techniques like deep breathing, yoga or meditation, this might be a good time to practise them.

sleep disturbance

Around 15 per cent of my ex-smokers experienced sleep problems in the form of wakefulness and disturbed dreams. Several had been using the 24-hour patches and found the vividness of the dreams too confronting or just exhausting. This problem has now been addressed with the 16-hour patches, which you take off at night. Other respondents reported dreaming about smoking – that's the one when you wake up in a panic convinced you have smoked. This is common, but isn't it great when you wake up properly and realise it was only a little old nightmare?

It's also quite normal to feel more tired than usual. This makes sense when you consider you are withdrawing from a stimulant. If it's at all practical, give in to the urge to sleep – except in your nightmares, you can't be tempted to smoke when you're unconscious! And each night's sleep moves you into another fresh day of your new life as a non-smoker.

appetite changes, weight gain

Experienced by more than three-quarters of women who stop smoking, this one is fully covered in Chapters 7 and 8. If you stopped smoking before reading this book and are still battling a weight problem, Chapter 16 is just for you.

coughing

A good sign, say the experts. It means your lungs are having a much-needed clear-out after years of mistreatment. You may not cough much at all or, alternatively, the coughing could continue for some time. Seek advice from your GP if you are worried.

mouth ulcers

This is a strange one, and not particularly common. I got them and so did a small number of my respondents. Thought by some to be caused by your body ridding itself of all those yukky toxins, and/or by your system being thrown into disarray with the sudden change of lifestyle! I heard another possible explanation recently from a woman who just happened to remark that if she ate too much sugar, in the form of sweets, she got a sore mouth. That makes sense to me.

Mouth ulcers are a short-term side-effect that is easy to fix. For free, try salt-water mouthwashes. One tea-spoon of kitchen salt dissolved in around 40 mls of warm boiled water and swished around your mouth for a couple of minutes a few times a day should do the trick. Otherwise, ask your pharmacist to recommend an antiseptic mouthwash. And talk to your GP if this doesn't work.

headaches

These could be caused by tension or changes to your blood pressure. Not a common side-effect – reported by just six per cent of my ex-smokers. Should be easy to fix with whatever you normally do to get rid of headaches. But if they last for more than a few days, see your doctor.

stomach pain/cramps

See Anxiety, on page 135. But don't ignore this for more than a few days, just in case it indicates a physical problem such as gastritis or a stomach ulcer. If it continues, see your GP.

spots

This short-term side-effect is probably due to your body adjusting to life without cigarettes and their attendant chemicals. Possibly also hormonal. Time should heal, as should exercise, good food, laughter. Most ex-smokers report clear, pink skin as a happy side-effect of quitting smoking.

lack of concentration

Nicotine is known to aid concentration, so it seems perfectly logical that when you remove it your concentration will be affected. Around half of my ex-smokers ticked yes to this one but by the time we got to the question, 'Which of the symptoms were the most difficult to overcome?', that particular symptom had all but vanished. There's not much you can do. Deep breathing might help the flow of oxygen to the brain, thereby aiding the thought process. But, hey, it could be psychological too! You're in the throes of a major lifestyle change, so it's no wonder you're not concentrating as well as usual! Anyway, it's all in a good cause. You can help yourself by putting aside anything that doesn't strictly need your concentration right now. Apart from that you'll just have to brazen it out.

mood swings, weepiness, anger, depression

More than three-quarters of my respondents suffered from one or a combination of this awesome foursome. And between them they caused as much havoc as the weight gain, irritability and cravings put together, although I have to say that the weight gain was still the longest-lasting of all the symptoms. All my ex-smokers found different ways to overcome their seesawing emotions, but it's disturbing to note that of the smokers who had tried unsuccessfully to quit, more than half gave these difficult emotions as a reason for lighting up again.

I got the lot with knobs on the day I switched down to the weakest patches, the 7 mg, and I'm sorry if that doesn't concur with the manufacturers' scientific research, but I'm just telling it the way it was for me. I kept a diary and it was the diary of a mad woman. I found myself swinging from elation to the depths of despair at the blink of an eye. And having not been much of a crier throughout my life, I swear I must have shed a lifetime of tears in the space of about a week. That's when I wasn't ranting and raving. Or hating the world one minute, then elevating ordinary events and people to mythical status the next. I was like a runaway train. Then one day I woke up feeling better; on the next day I was better still, and on the one after that I was back in control, human again. And the duration of this madness? Eight days.

There seems to be so little interest in why women experience a whole host of withdrawal symptoms that men appear not to. Even those who are sympathetic tend to assume these symptoms are strictly psychological. We're told we're going through a grieving process for the loss of an old friend. We're told we may have been using cigarettes to cope with stress or push down difficult feelings, so when we take the nicotine away it unlocks the floodgates. We're told counselling might help. I think all these things are probably true up to a point. But are they the whole story? And how are we supposed to function normally while it's all going on?

One expert who has been looking closely at this

problem is Professor Neil Grunberg, and he believes the mood swings and other emotional problems we experience when we stop smoking are connected to the serotonin in the brain and other hormones that affect the emotional state. He cites some as-yet-unpublished studies in the US which put the female sex hormone progesterone in the frame. His solution for women suffering severe ongoing emotional problems after quitting smoking would be to prescribe Prozac or one of the other new breed of anti-depressant drugs. One such drug is Zyban (see page 104), which he says is proving a very popular smoking cessation aid in the States.

shut up and lay it on the line!

Of course, if you are in the throes of all this, you are probably not in the least bit interested in academic arguments. So here's what may help:

- Do something physical. Nicotine affects the happy hormones dopamine and serotonin. So does exercise, any kind of exercise. Even a brisk walk or vacuuming the house will make you feel better. Not fabulous perhaps, not today anyway, but definitely better.

- Do something that will make you laugh. See a funny movie, a comedy show on TV, phone or get together with people who make you laugh. Laughter is the best antidote to the blues.

- Alternatively, give yourself something to cry about. Have a night in alone, put on the headphones and play all the music that has a direct line to your tear ducts. Having a good cry from time to time is good for you. It's like clearing out cupboards.

- Then again, you could play any music that makes you feel good. Better still, go out and listen to some live music. Wait a minute. What am I saying? One of the worst things for me about giving up smoking is that I love live music. And where does all the good stuff happen? That's right. In smoky pubs and clubs. Look, just do what feels right. My feeling is, if you love music – any kind of music – and you've got a sense of humour, there is nothing life can throw at you that you can't cope with, and that includes nicotine withdrawal symptoms.

- If you've been using alcohol to take the edge off the feelings and you're now spiralling into a pit, try to stop drinking for a few days. Alcohol can make you feel great but it can also make you depressed. Cutting it out should speed up your recovery. In fact, women who don't drink seem to find the whole process of giving up smoking a lot easier than those of us who do.

- Find a friendly shoulder to cry on. Call one of your support team, or you could call the national Quit line on 131 848 and ask to be put through to a counsellor. Talking to a stranger in this situation wouldn't be my first choice. But I have an axe to grind. When I called the Quit line, in the throes of withdrawal, I opened the conversation by saying: 'I've just quit smoking and I'm using the patches . . .' The voice on the end of the phone interrupted pompously: 'If you're using the patches, you haven't quit smoking, have you?' I'm told things have changed since then. Call the number when you're feeling good, and find out what services are available in your state. I'm told the phone lines are staffed by trained counsellors who are supposed to be supportive and non-judgemental. If you call them and this is not your experience, I'd like to hear about it.

■ If the mood swings and other emotional problems are too hard to handle, go and see your doctor and discuss the possibility of getting some anti-depressants. If your doctor is not sympathetic, find one who is. If you have to, remind your doctor that until recently, you were one of the four million or so tax-paying, law-abiding citizens who contributed $4.6 billion worth of revenue to the community. You'd like some of it back, please!

■ But don't feel too sorry for yourself. Save some of that pity for those who really need it – the folk who are still smoking. They are going to have to do all this one day. You'll be feeling great sooner than you think. Just like the women in the next chapter who went through everything you're going through and came out the other end nicotine free and smiling, and with self-esteem to spare.

Giving up smoking has been the best thing I have done in my life to date. Cigarettes ruled me totally. Looking back, it was very sad and pathetic. Even when I was broke I had to have them. I smoked rather than ate a meal. Now I am in control of what I do. I am more assertive and I am enjoying good health. Why didn't I stop sooner? *Ann, 35, a smoker for 17 years. Used to smoke 40–60 a day. Hasn't smoked for 22 months.*

The only thing I regret about the past is the length of it. If I had to live again I'd make all the same mistakes only sooner.

TALLULAH BANKHEAD

14

The smoke screen clears

CONSCIOUS THAT 'NORMAL' IS such a relative state, I asked my ex-smokers, 'Roughly how long after quitting did you start to feel "normal", i.e. free of withdrawal symptoms?' Three to four weeks was the shortest time given and two years the longest. Around half said it had taken between one and three months, while a quarter reported it had taken from four months to a year for life to return to normal.

Those who reported feeling the pinch for longer were not talking about 4 to 12 months of full-on withdrawal symptoms. It might just be a moment or two of emptiness, a vague longing, sometimes a strong but fleeting physical craving for nicotine, or just the feeling that it would be nice to sit down and have a cigarette, to enjoy the ritual of smoking. These symptoms were usually brief and more likely to be interspersed with feelings of sheer joy at being a non-smoker. I agree. It's also worth noting that for many of us, this is our first experience of being an adult without an addiction! It's no wonder we need time to properly get used to this!

Weight gain was the worst, although the weepiness and depression were probably the most unpleasant at the time. I actually had two days off work because I couldn't cope. I was either going to cry or kill somebody. I feel strong now. *Sophie, 27, a smoker for seven years, smoked 15–20 a day. Hasn't smoked for 29 days.*

Of my ex-smokers who had not smoked for six months or more, three-quarters reported just one remaining withdrawal symptom: weight gain. The rest said that symptoms such as anger, irritability, weepiness and a feeling of emptiness were still hanging around. When I went back over their questionnaires I discovered, not exactly to my surprise, that these were women in their 40s and 50s, smokers since their early teens, who had been heavily dependent on nicotine until they'd found the courage to stop.

I felt really bad for the first ten days. I couldn't even drive the car. By three months I could laugh again and felt a lot better but I was still crying regularly. By 12 months, heaps better. *Julie, 40, a smoker for 20 years, smoked 25–50 'real' (15 mg) cigarettes a day.*

Anger was the feeling I pushed down the most with cigarettes. After I quit I'd feel it and try to release energy and deal with it. *Janey, 45, a smoker for 29 years, smoked 25 a day. Hasn't smoked for two and a half years. Felt 'normal' after three months.*

Some of these women are battling a host of demons – an unhappy or abusive childhood and its insidious knock-on effects, a childhood trauma like the loss of a parent, problems with their sexuality (the main problem usually being people's attitude to their sexuality), unhappy adult relationships. Plus all the regular, everyday problems that everyone has to face: work pressure, relationship pressure, parenting pressure, financial pressure, worrying about the state of the world pressure. And they've removed an important part of their armoury, a drug which peps them up, calms them down and without which their coping mechanism has gone haywire. And another possibility for the women in their 40s and 50s is that they may also be pre-menopausal. (In fact, if you are in that age-group, any ongoing emotional problems, especially dramatic mood swings, might be worth checking out with your doctor in case they are hormonal. Don't forget to let her or him know you have recently stopped smoking.)

But no matter how strong the withdrawal symptoms may be, these women and many more like them managed to stay off the cigarettes. They have been non-smokers for four months, six months, nine months, a year, two years. They are women like you and women like me. And although they may be having their ups and downs, they know what I know, and what you are probably already finding out: being a non-smoker just *gets better every day*.

After more than two years of not smoking, I still

have the odd withdrawal symptom. The weepiness has never completely gone away. So many things can bring a tear to my eye these days: a group of kindergarten kids singing 'Away in a Manger', an old favourite song, an act of kindness, an act of wickedness, a schmaltzy scene in a film, a flawless blue sky over Sydney Harbour, a smile from a cute baby in the street, a hug from my own cute baby – and I've learnt to live with it. It's probably not very healthy never to cry anyway. Nowadays I regard being able to shed a tear or two after years of never crying as a sign that I'm alive.

Irritability is another. There's no doubt I'm crankier than I used to be and more likely to let someone know if they've stepped over the line. And I wasn't entirely passive to begin with. But where I once used to reach for a cigarette to dispel strong pissed-off feelings in order to keep the peace, I now have to deal with those feelings unaided, and some days I'm better at it than others.

Anger's a toughie. It's a powerful emotion that repels and frightens people. Especially women's anger. Unless we are able to dilute it with humour, it's difficult to find an outlet for it or gain any sympathy. How much anger is socially acceptable is anybody's guess. It depends on the kind of life you lead and the people around you.

I don't believe that self-centred, ill-mannered people should feel free to blunder around in your life oblivious to the effects of their behaviour. On the other hand, we can't go around letting off steam left, right and centre however justified we might feel. Apart from anything else, the root cause of our anger is usually far away or otherwise untouchable, so it often gets misdirected and let loose on someone who doesn't deserve it.

I think we have to set our own boundaries to decide how much anger is too much. Or how much sadness is too much. If people who once enjoyed our company are suddenly not returning our calls, or making one lame excuse after another not to see us; I don't mean just one person, I mean several. Or if our loved ones are tiptoeing around us all the time trying to keep us pacified beyond reasonable limits, then it's fair to assume that the removal of nicotine has exposed more than just a few raw nerves, and it may be time to seek professional help.

But don't go rushing off to the doctor for Prozac or to counselling the first time you bawl someone out or burst into tears. Give yourself at least six months to adjust to life without cigarettes. Because I still believe that by simply getting free of this damned drug addiction you'll be taking the most important step you can take towards feeling whole and in control, which includes being able to handle life's inevitable irritations.

People used to hate me

and now they like me,

not that I give a damn

either way.

CHER

15

The sweet smell of success – don't blow it

Quitting smoking, like any other complex human activity, is an enigmatic business. I can't give you a thermometer to gauge your ex-smoker status, but you will know when it has happened. You will stop thinking about ciga-rettes; you will no longer even feel smug, just normal. You will become an ex-smoker when cigarettes cease to have any relevance in your life. Researchers . . . usually define successful ex-smokers as those who are still off cigarettes a year after they quit. But this is a somewhat arbi-trary threshold . . . I, for one, knew that after I had weathered the first two months there was no question of ever going back to cigarettes.

BOBBIE JACOBSON, *BEATING THE LADYKILLERS*.

It must be great to be as certain of your status as a non-smoker as Bobbie Jacobson after just two months. Perhaps you are. If so, that's fantastic. But what if you're not? What if you're suffering a crisis of confidence? You feel restless, anxious, a bit miserable and you still think a lot about smoking. In fact, when you see someone lighting up, you get a feeling of . . . well, smoker envy. You wish you could get back to your familiar old pal, nicotine.

If you've survived the first four to six weeks as a non-smoker, the worst is well and truly over and you have every reason to be confident that you can live without cigarettes for good. Your emotions might still be a bit topsy-turvy, but you will never again feel as bad as you felt in the first few weeks. Except, of course, if you give in now and start smoking. What keeps most people going is just one thought: 'I don't ever want to go through that again.' The same applies to those of you who are not yet over the worst. Hang in there. Do what you have to do to stop yourself smoking. Because every day you don't smoke will be easier than the one before. Anyway, you'll hate yourself if you give in now – you know you will, because chances are you've been here before.

No one can put a time limit on how long it will take your body and brain to get used to the new non-smoking you. But the longer you were a smoker, the more time you will need to adjust. Meanwhile, because nicotine is a widely available, perfectly legal drug the temptation to smoke is all around. I asked my ex-smokers if they still get the urge to smoke and 84 per cent said yes. The good news is that the overwhelming majority reported the urge to be 'mild and it passes quickly'. Those who said the urge to smoke was strong enough to cause distress had all been ex-smokers for less than three months. Yet even they reported that most of these urges passed quickly.

What, I asked, are the circumstances that make you want to smoke? The most powerful trigger was being in the company of smokers. So it won't come as a surprise to anyone to learn that around three-quarters of ex-smokers admit they try to avoid places where people are likely to be smoking.

While being around smokers is the number one trigger, hot on its heels is drinking alcohol. And it goes without saying that triggers one and two combined are a dangerous duo indeed. Number three trigger is stress, with pressure at work leading the charge and family stress not far behind. Next comes drinking coffee and smoking marijuana. And finally there's curiosity, which may never have killed any self-respecting cat but can be extremely hazardous to the newly reformed smoker. Let's look at some of the pitfalls in more detail.

the company of smokers

I asked my ex-smokers: 'Why do you avoid smokers and smoky atmospheres?' Because we hate the smell, said about a quarter. It makes us want to smoke, said the rest.

I no longer tolerate passive smoking having made the enormous effort to stop. I quit polluting my

lungs so everyone else has to stop polluting them too! *Justine, 32, a smoker for 14 years. Smoked 20–50 a day. Hasn't smoked for 18 months.*

I avoid smokers because I really do find the smell obnoxious. But I also avoid smokers because if I'm having a good night and I've had a few drinks, and there's a pack on the table, I don't trust myself not to smoke. *Olivia, 42, a smoker for 26 years. Hasn't smoked for 16 months.*

Before I quit smoking I used to fantasise about what sort of person I would be as an ex-smoker. And of course, I was never going to be the sort who had made my life difficult from the moment the government declared open season on smokers. You know the type of ex-smoker I mean. The type who invites you to their house knowing you're a smoker, acts surprised when you ask if you can smoke, makes a huge performance of finding an ashtray, then makes it clear they'd prefer you to smoke outside. Or the kind of ex-smoker who sits near you in a restaurant, or anywhere where smoking is permitted, then gets their kicks by delivering black looks, much tutting, and much agitated waving of the hands if any of your smoke wafts in their direction. Or everybody's favourite: the 'social' smoker, who reckons she's 'kicked the habit' when we know the only habit she's kicked is actually buying cigarettes. I have had so many tense times in the company of such individuals, I was determined to be a model of decorum in my new life as a non-smoker.

And I swear I tried really hard to live up to this warm and fuzzy image I had of myself. In my house ashtrays were produced for friends with the minimum of fuss. *And* they were invited to smoke inside, in comfort. And because I used to need to smoke in between courses at meal times, I always offered my smoking guests an inter-course smoke break. I wanted my visitors to have a nice time and smokers who are stressing because they can't smoke never have a nice time.

The cigarette that put me back on the road to re-addiction was in a pack left behind by a friend who had spent an evening at my house. It wasn't the first time I'd been tempted to smoke and it wasn't her fault that I picked that night to give in to the temptation. But I'd been breathing in cigarette smoke all evening and by the time she left, the nicotine had wheedled its way back into my bloodstream and my body wanted more. And the packet was sitting there. And it was my old brand. And my partner, my conscience, was fast asleep in bed. That's not an excuse for my weakness but it is the reason why my house is now smoke free.

I have found that people who have never smoked are generally tolerant to cigarette smoke because they have no personal axe to grind (although recently I've noticed this group becoming more and more vocal about cigarette smoke and not wanting to be around it). People who've quit can, for the sake of self-preservation, be quite intolerant. Once you no longer need to smoke, you no longer need to avoid your smoking friends. But be aware that some of us may never be completely delivered from temptation.

alcohol

When not in cahoots with cigarette smoke, alcohol – in moderation – is usually fine. Otherwise it can be a bit dangerous. Alcohol is a chemical trigger, added to which is the problem of poor judgement which we all know usually sets in after the third or fourth drink. Combined with the easy availability of cigarettes, especially that bloody pack that's always on the table in front of you on these occasions, the temptation can sometimes prove too much.

Surprisingly, your frame of mind seems to make no difference to the timing of these unwanted urges. You are just as likely to want to smoke when you are having a nice, relaxing time as when you are stressed to hell. In fact, in my experience, the most dangerous moments for ex-smokers are when we're out having fun and life is currently pretty good. Because we feel happy we make the mistake of thinking we can handle it.

What happens next is you fixate on the nearest pack and start mentally weighing up the pros and cons of having 'just one'. And although you may not be drunk, your judgement is impaired enough for you to believe you can have 'just one cigarette' and be over it by the morning. And the first time you do it, that's how it might seem. I had 'just one cigarette' after a nice meal in a restaurant. I felt vaguely stupid the next morning (and my throat and lungs hurt), but I then went for weeks without thinking about smoking. Which at the time I thought proved I'd learnt how to be a 'social' smoker. In fact, all it really proved was that I should get out more. Because the next time I was out for dinner, again with smokers, I had 'just one cigarette'. And that night, I enjoyed it so much I had a second. Then on the next occasion, I bought my smoking chum a pack and smoked two or three with a clear conscience. And in a frighteningly short space of time, I was a full-on, full-time smoker again.

coffee

Nicotine, a stimulant, is known to subdue the stimulatory effects of the caffeine in coffee. (For some reason it doesn't seem to have the same effect with tea, perhaps because of the lower levels of caffeine.) So if as a smoker you were used to drinking a lot of coffee and you try to maintain that same intake after you've quit, you may find yourself getting the jitters. The solution is to cut back on coffee, and your body, wonderful machine that it is, may help you by letting you know it doesn't want as much coffee as it used to. A number of my ex-smokers reported this happening and it happened to me too. As a smoker I used to drink three or four mugs of strong, black filter coffee a day, including one after dinner at night. Now I'm down to two a day, and the only one I *need* is that first wake-up cup of the day with breakfast. I didn't make a decision to do this. It just happened.

About ten per cent of my ex-smokers said sitting down with a cup of coffee triggered the urge to smoke. But these urges were not strong and no one reported coffee as a problem.

smoking marijuana

I was once a big fan of the wacky baccy, but it's another vice I've given up. Or rather, like various other youth-ful pursuits – such as the ability to stay up all night and still function the next day – it's given me up. I stopped enjoying joints so I decided to save my money for the things I do enjoy.

I've known many marijuana smokers who don't smoke tobacco and who roll joints with herbs and goodness knows what else. Some tobacco-free joints taste like they've been rolled with old socks. I also know of people who smoke marijuana with tobacco but who wouldn't smoke a cigarette if you paid them. However, these are not ex-smokers. They are people who have never been addicted to nicotine. I don't know any ex-nicotine addicts who can smoke marijuana with tobacco without getting hooked on tobacco again.

curiosity and nostalgia

You've been off the cigarettes for a while. Your lungs feel good. You feel good. You know you don't need to smoke any more. As Bobbie Jacobson says, you no longer even feel smug about it, just normal. You love being a non-smoker. But the novelty has worn off. No one is making a fuss of you now, and because you feel so healthy you're forgetting how your mouth, throat and lungs used to feel, and how smelly your hair and clothes once were.

Have you noticed, too, how smoking is becoming fashionable in movies and on TV again? And in the old movies everyone smoked. So while direct cigarette advertising, in the days when it was permitted, didn't change your smoking habits one iota, seeing your favourite movie or TV star puffing away makes it seem sexy. There's no doubt about it – the ritual of lighting up a cigarette, putting it to the lips and drawing the smoke deep can be very sensuous indeed – especially when the smoker is gorgeous and getting paid a fortune to make it look that way. At these times I often find myself watching them intently and almost feeling the surge of happy hormones as the smoke hits the back of the throat.

This is a dangerous phase of your new life as a non-smoker. You are curious to know what cigarettes taste like after all this time. And that movie you've just seen has made you feel nostalgic. As I said before, you are suffering from smoker envy. The nostalgia part is easy to deal with. Look the word up in the dictionary: it means a yearning, a sickness, something to be got over.

As for the curiosity, allow me to satisfy it for you so you don't have to sabotage your hard-won status as a non-smoker. If it is only a short time, say a few months, since you last smoked, that 'just one cigarette', if you are nuts enough to have it, will taste great and you'll get a real buzz from it. I can almost guarantee you'll enjoy that cigarette. If it's been a long while since you smoked, the cigarette itself will probably taste disgusting but you'll still get a buzz from the nicotine. Either way, you have just stepped onto the slippery slope back to addiction. How do I know? How do you think I know? I am happy for you to learn from my mistake!

Of course, some of you may be able to leave it at 'just one', your curiosity satisfied. But what's more likely is that you'll go back for seconds. And, on the next occasion you reach for a cigarette, you can take it as read that this versatile drug has got you in its powerful grip again. It might take days, weeks, months or (as in the case of a friend of mine who at social gatherings used to ask if she could 'light your cigarette for you') a couple of years to become hooked again. But it's a matter of *when*, not *if*. I do not believe for one minute that those of us who were once addicted to nicotine can ever be casual or social smokers.

If we do give in to the temptation, we'll be back to the misery and anxiety of being smokers again before we know it. And as well as living daily with the sheer inconvenience of needing to smoke, that lack of control over your life, the niggling feeling of unease that this next cigarette might be the one that triggers one of those horrible-sounding diseases . . . almost as bad is having to contemplate going through the withdrawal process all over again. I've been there, done that, and more than likely so have you. I'm not doing it again. Neither are my ex-smokers. I asked them 'Do you believe you are a non-smoker for life?' and all but a handful said yes. Of the rest, some said they were too close to their last cigarette – less than three months – to be that confident, while one or two reckoned if they're still alive at 75 they might take it up again. Fair enough. Personally, I'm hoping that by the time I reach 75 there might be a recreational drug on the market that delivers a lot more pleasure with far fewer side-effects!

*I worry about scientists
discovering that lettuce
has been fattening
all along.*

ERMA BOMBECK

16

More weighty matters – it's never too late

CONGRATULATIONS ON GETTING FREE of the weed! Doesn't it feel great? It's almost like being reborn. I suppose that sounds a bit dramatic, but for those of us who have puffed our way through our teens and several decades of adulthood, that's exactly how it feels to be a new non-smoker.

Now having been wondrously reborn, I expect you'd like to see your body restored to its pre-rebirth shape. In fact, if you've been a non-smoker for some time, I bet you'd settle for something that was even *close* to your pre-rebirth shape, wouldn't you? Well you can. And it's going to be a whole lot easier than giving up smoking. Which you've already achieved. By using a stricter version of the strategy for ex-smokers-to-be set out in Chapter 8, I lost 6.5 kilograms (1 stone) in 12 weeks. That's a kilo every two weeks. All I did was eat less and move more by reducing the level of fat in my regular diet and introducing some moderate – and mostly free – exercise into my life.

A word of warning: if you are pregnant or breast-feeding, taking regular medication or have any ongoing health problems at all, talk to your doctor before following this. Although reducing your fat intake in your diet and increasing the amount of exercise in your life is pretty standard advice these days, this is not a professional weight-loss program. What I am offering is an informal weight-reduction strategy that worked for me.

Although far more sympathetic to the problem of weight gain than most experts on smoking and nicotine, Neil Grunberg cautions that some of the long-term weight gain we experience when we give up smoking can be attributed to subtle changes in our eating habits that *are* within our control. 'It is not purely metabolic,' he says. 'It's to do with the sweet and carbohydrate shift, which *is* metabolic. But because of the metabolic shift, you are probably changing the distribution of the nutrients you are eating without realising it.'

In other words, if you're not careful, your metabolic handful of jelly beans can start sneaking into your diet in other ways. 'This means a little more mayonnaise here, a little more sugar there and you probably don't notice it,' Grunberg says. 'If you kept a careful record of your diet, you'd be amazed at the variants. If I start eating raisin toast for breakfast instead of a good wholegrain cereal, I can be making a shift in hundreds of calories a day without realising it.'

If you've only recently stopped smoking and you're still gaining weight *and* suffering other withdrawal symptoms, my heart goes out to you. I know exactly what you're going through. And so do most of the women (and plenty of men) who have successfully given up smoking. Your body feels like it's on an unruly automatic pilot over which you have no control. But please try to stick with not smoking. And until the withdrawal symptoms ease up, don't try to lose weight. It might take three or four months of not smoking for you to feel confident about tackling any weight gain. For some of you it might be less, while others might need longer.

If I'd realised half of what was going on when my body was relentlessly expanding, I would have been looking at a strategy like this after about four months of not smoking. By then, I was feeling reasonably strong and I could have saved myself many months of bewilderment plus the cost of larger clothes. But hindsight is a wonderful thing . . . as is the cliché 'better late than never'.

Don't make the mistake of thinking that you'll get your weight under control if you start smoking again. It doesn't work like that. You'd have to smoke a lot of cigarettes over a long period to notice any weight reduction. The withdrawal symptoms would be long gone by then. Anyway, what about all your hard work so far? You'd have to go through it all again eventually. How do I know? How do you think I know? Another of life's little lessons learnt the hard way! But you don't have to learn it the hard way. Just stay focused on being a non-smoker. And try not to feel too sorry for yourself, because guess what? You don't smoke. So get back to your jelly-bean jar and you can read the rest of this chapter when you feel more in control.

Those of you who are over the other withdrawal symptoms sufficiently to tackle this last hurdle probably have a pretty good idea of how much weight you want to lose. Your first step is the same as in Chapter 8. If you haven't already got one, you'll need to invest in a calculator and a fat counter. The shelves of your local bookstore are probably groaning with them, so take your pick. But for around $5 each, the two mentioned on page 81 between them cover most of the food and beverages you're likely to come across in Australia, including branded foods. Both also contain heaps of helpful nutritional advice that is well worth reading. You probably know quite a bit of it already, but I found this a good time to refresh my memory.

Next, choosing three gastronomically unremark-able days in your life, write down everything that passes your lips, together with its fat content, and add up each day's total. Use the middle total to determine your daily fat intake. You could do this for longer if you want to but three days should be enough to give you a good idea of your average regular intake.

Here's where your strategy changes from that of the pre-quitting smokers who just want to maintain their weight. In order to lose a kilo a fortnight – with week-ends off – I reduced my fat intake to between 25 and 35 grams a day and kept my kilojoule intake to around 6300 (1500 calories) a day. I admit I was sometimes bored but I was never hungry between meals. As I said in Chapter 8, I also added around 45 minutes of exercise to my life whenever I could. This mostly involved brisk walking two or three times a week and a pathetic amount of strictly recreational swimming. Eat less, move more. It really is that simple. But this was not a major lifestyle change for me. I customised my weight-loss plan to suit my life and not the other way round.

If you are feeling more ambitious but still don't fancy the gym you could even get yourself a personal trainer. No, I know you're not Madonna. You don't have to be. If you live in or near a town or city there are professional Amazons out there who, for around $60 a session, will work out a personalised program to suit any location – from your backyard to the park – that you can ultimately go off and do by yourself. So then it costs nothing. So if your idea of exercise is a brisk walk around your local streets and park a couple of times a week, one of these extremely fit human beings can add an extra frisson of excitement by identifying some steps for you to run up en route, or giving you ten minutes of heart-rate-raising exercise to do on the grass. This industry is as yet unregu-lated in Australia so ensure she or he has at least completed a recognised fitness leader's course at a TAFE college. As always, a personal recommendation is best, or look in your local paper or call your local gym.

no sad loss

I started my weight-loss effort with a few advantages: the first was that I began in summer, a time for eating lighter food and less of it. Also I can live without cakes et al, butter and cream; I can happily get by on at least three meatless meals each week; I don't eat much junk/processed food; and I don't like breakfast, at least not your everyday rushing-out-the-door-for-work type breakfast. I know the prevailing advice is to always eat a 'good' breakfast, but again the experts are seeing humanity the way they'd like us to be and asking us to make lifestyle changes that may not suit us. Although I'm not a big breakfast eater, I have to eat something in the morning. So, for this weight-reduction strategy I pinched an idea from the famous *Fit For Life* book and started eating only fresh fruit before midday, and it works fine for me.

Working against me was that I love cheese, and the more flavoursome the cheese the higher the fat content. Because I don't eat a lot of meat, I used to eat cheese most days so having to cut it back was my biggest sacrifice. Also on my hard-to-live-without list were nuts (very good for you, but surprisingly high in fat), avocados (ditto) and generous spoonfuls of real mayonnaise and olive oil. And I like chocolate and Kettle chips, especially the chilli ones. But having carried all this blubber around with me for months I was very motivated and seeing the needle on the scale going steadily downward, plus having to keep tightening my belt on my 'fat jeans', made these small sacrifices worthwhile.

On the following pages you'll find some tried and trusted hints and short-cuts. There is also a list of regular sports and mundane activities together with the kilojoules they burn. If you're not already familiar with all this stuff and you want to know more, just browse the health section in any bookshop and you'll find a whole host of weight-loss plans and exercise strategies written by people far more qualified than I am. But if at any point it all gets too hard, seek advice from your doctor. Or, if you can afford it, consider joining a well-established weight-loss group like Weightwatchers or Jenny Craig. You'll get professional help and advice on how to lose weight, plus some morale-boosting group empathy and support. And no matter how desperate you feel, avoid any diet that involves being hungry. Ditto 'miracle' weight-loss programs or pills and potions. The rule of thumb is if it sounds too good to be true, it probably is.

creative counting

I'm sure many of you could recite some or all of the following information in your sleep, so feel free to skip it. But if you're like me and haven't done any weight-watching since the days when going on a diet meant furiously counting kilojoules and starving half to death on the latest fad diets, read on.

- **Fat Facts:** Fats in food comes in three different types known as saturated, mono-saturated and polyunsaturated. *Saturated* fats are the tastiest, the hardest to resist and, wouldn't you know it, the baddies for people trying to control their weight. Found in meat products, solid fat for cooking, full-cream dairy products and many processed foods such as cakes, pastries and biscuits. Vegetable fats and oils used in processed foods are usually saturated fats, too. *Mono-unsaturated* fats and *polyunsaturated* fats are lower in fat than animal products, but still fairly high. And they are also high in kilojoules. Found in foods such as oils and margarines, nuts, avocados, sesame seeds.

Top tip: Substitute fat foods with foods that are high in fibre. They're tasty, healthy and they make you feel full.

■ A significant amount of fat can be eliminated without you even noticing it's gone, simply by altering the method of preparation or cooking. Instead of frying fish, chicken or vegetables – steam, microwave, grill, barbecue or bake them in the oven, brushed with a little good quality oil (extra virgin olive oil is best). For flavour use garlic, herbs (fresh or dried), Tabasco, Worcestershire sauce. A half-breast of roast chicken, without skin, cooked with herbs, garlic and moistened with just a light brushing of oil has around 3.8 grams of fat. If you leave on the skin and roast it in butter the fat content leaps to 12.4 grams.

■ Meat is fat city, especially the cheaper cuts. One average Aussie beef sausage weighs in at a bouncing 17.5 grams! That's more than half a dieter's daily allowance. I love sausages but I left them alone while I was trying to lose weight. Kinder cuts for carnivores include trim lamb steak (an average steak of 100 grams contains 4.5 grams of fat), skinless chicken or pork loin chops (3.5 grams each). Trim any excess fat off the meat or ask your butcher to do it.

Top tip: Try to make at least two main meals a week meat free.

■ Try to spend some quality time at your local supermarket (don't laugh – I'm serious) and stop at some of the shelves you'd normally walk straight past. You know the ones I mean! You may find some pleasant surprises that can help you over a hurdle or two.

Top tip: Lite and Light don't necessarily mean low in fat or kilojoules. Food labels can make interesting reading.

■ Experiment with low-fat alternatives to high-fat foods. There's no point in pretending they taste as good as the real thing, because they don't. But some are better than others and better than nothing at all. Those that passed my taste test include: low-fat milk, several brands of low-fat yoghurt, Weightwatchers' lemon and pepper mayo; Bodalla low-fat cheddar and Cracker Barrel light; fat-reduced ham off the bone; Bulla low-fat ice-cream; pretzels, Grissini bread sticks, popcorn, rice crackers. Those that didn't: skim milk; low-fat cottage cheese (why bother?); all the other low-fat cheeses; commercial oil-free salad dressing.

■ **Say cheese!** Cheese fans like me must resign ourselves to steering clear of our favourite high-fat
cheeses until after the weight has gone. Instead,
find a deli that sells great Parmesan. It's compara-
tively low in fat (3.1 grams per grated tablespoon),
makes a great topping for pasta with nothing else
added, and you can use it as a substitute for cheddar in many dishes. Ditto mozzarella (2.3 grams
per tablespoon).
Top tip: The fat content of cheese is lowered when
it is grated – it's bulkier so you use less.

■ Regular cottage cheese is low in fat (1.6 grams of
fat per 30 grams) and is very versatile. You can substitute it in dishes that normally require higher fat
cheeses like cream cheese or ricotta. Or turn it into
an okay topping for jacket potatoes by flavouring
it to within an inch of its life with any (or all, if you
wish) of the following: chilli; salsa; any fresh herbs
(chives, parsley and dill are good); mustard;
Tabasco; Worcestershire sauce. Or use it to bulk
out a green salad. It goes well with tuna or hard-
boiled egg. I fell back on this a number of times
when I'd overdone it at lunch and I needed a low-
fat dinner. Or if I was planning to overdo it at
dinner and needed a low-fat lunch.

■ Want some good news? Alcohol contains no fat.
The bad news? It has a fair amount of sugar and
can make you want to smoke, so caution is advised
after the second drink.

- **Low-fat, high-fibre goodies:** pasta, bread, potatoes, rice, beans, fresh and dried fruit, plus moderate amounts of fish and lean meat with the skin removed.

- **No-fat munchie material:** for those moments when you need to stave off a between-meals hunger pang (or a sugar craving) and a raw carrot stick just won't do, go for a sugar hit. A small handful of jelly beans, boiled sweets, chewing gum, peppermints, Life Savers, marshmallows, fruit pastilles (or jubes) will set you back around 420 kjs (100 cals). Or try a plain water cracker spread with a little jam. Alternatively, if you want to avoid wasting kilojoules on a sugar hit, Neil Grunberg recommends a slice of bread or a piece of celery, sprinkled with sugar substitute. It's a thought but I haven't been game to try it yet!

- **My favourite weight-loss tip:** for those of us who can take or leave breakfast, eating only fresh fruit before lunch means a no-fuss breakfast, plus the chance to save fat foods for more enjoyable meals. Bananas are especially good because they are filling. I've stuck with this new habit. On an average morning I eat at least one large or two small bananas, an apple or pear and/or a handful of grapes or strawberries or whatever else is looking good at the fruit shop.

- Try to resist the urge to weigh yourself too often. It's tempting, I know, but you'll drive yourself crazy. I started off doing it weekly (on the same day every week) but switched to fortnightly the first time I got on the scales and nothing had happened, even though I had been diligently fat-counting. What soon became clear was that sometimes I was losing a kilogram every two weeks rather than half this amount each week.

■ Don't be in too much of a hurry to lose weight, but don't get too relaxed about it either. I got sloppy and started having *long* weekends off for good behaviour and generally falling off the wagon. The result was that my weight loss stalled before I'd quite reached my goal. I got serious again, but by then boredom – and winter – had set in.

turning the corner

If you get halfway towards your goal and find the weight loss has ground to a halt, it might be a good time to stop and have a think. You could find you've forgotten why the ultimate goal was so important in the first place. After all, you've given up smoking and you've lost some weight. Not as much as you wanted to at the beginning, but you're starting to quite like what you see in the mirror. That clear skin and those bright eyes look good too, don't they?

To the question 'How long did it take you to return to your former weight', the most common response – from more than three-quarters of the women – was 'I haven't yet'. But while over half of these were still strug-gling to shed those recalcitrant kilos, and clearly a bit depressed about it, the rest didn't seem unhappy at all.

> **I became depressed, angry, then went to Jenny Craig and eventually lost ten kilos.** *Suzie, 41, a smoker for 21 years. Hasn't smoked for 18 months. Gained around 20 kilos and is still about 10 kilos more than she was as a smoker.*

So what's Suzie doing about the other ten kilos?

> **I try and exercise a bit and I still watch my fat con-tent but the weight is not so much of a problem any more. I'm over it now. I feel strong. In control.**

Suzie is an acquaintance. Unknowingly, we quit smok-ing within a few months of one another. We met up at a birthday party at what was the lowest point for both of us in our new lives as non-smokers. I was very visi-bly overweight and so was she. I spotted her first and hardly recognised this bloated, unhappy figure as the cheerful, sociable Suzie I'd met at many similar gather-ings in the past. In fact, we hardly recognised one another. For most of the party we stood unhappily in a corner with our drinks, looking enviously at our smok-ing friends, swapping nicotine withdrawal symptoms. And we whinged. Boy, did we whinge! Mostly about the sheer scale of the weight gain and how it had caught us totally by surprise.

Some months later, we met up again at another social event. As we approached one another our smiles got broader. 'You're looking well', I remarked. 'You don't look so bad yourself', she replied. What understatement! We both looked great and what's more, we knew it. And we felt great too! Suzie had lost more than half her original weight gain and gained back some self-esteem . . . and the sparkle in her eyes. I, too, had lost just over half of my eventual gain of 13 kilos and found some sense of achievement. We sipped our drinks, started to chat and joke and swap stories of our efforts to take control of our wayward metabolisms. But this time, and here is the best bit, we were not looking enviously at our smoking sisters. We were over it! One or two of our friends who were smoking remarked how much they envied us for being free.

Neither of us had returned to our former sylph-like selves, but we'd both turned a corner. Our modest fat-watching strategy had paid off. So too had that equally modest exercise. With these good habits now well entrenched our weight had stabilised. We were back in control of our bodies at last. Meanwhile, my compulsion to be seven and a half stone again, the weight I was throughout my 20s and most of my 30s, seems to have passed. I quite like what I see in the mirror now. And I need a bit of a break from plain salad sandwiches and low-fat cheese. But most important of all is that I am a non-smoker. And it's brilliant.

As I said at the beginning of this book, I am not a

doctor, or a psychologist or a smoking cessation expert. What I am is an ex-smoker who found that the reality of giving up smoking – for me, and for the many, many women I talked to – didn't quite concur with much of the prevailing advice and information. What I have written here, though unashamedly subjective, frequently anecdotal and at times emotional, is an attempt to redress the balance. For those of you who are just starting out, I wish you every success in your quest to quit smoking and I hope my book makes a difference. Good luck to you all! I'd love to hear how you get on. You can write to me at PO Box 1760, Rozelle, NSW 2039.

A SPORTING CHANCE

Activity	Kilojoules/calories used per minute, based on a person weighing 60 kilos (or 9.5 stone)	
Aerobics	27.3kjs	6.5 cals
Basketball	35.7	8.5
Badminton	25.2	6.0
Cleaning house	16.4	3.9
Cooking dinner	12.2	2.9
Cycling (15 kms p h)	24.0	5.7
Dancing (disco/jazz)	14.7	3.5
Football	33.0	7.8
Gardening (raking)	14.7	3.5
Golf	21.0	5.0
Gymnastics	16.8	4.0
Hockey	19.8	4.7
Horse-riding (trotting)	33.2	7.9
Judo	46.2	11.0
Playing piano	25.0	10.5
Rowing (machine – fast)	27.5	6.5
Running (average speed)	50.5	12.0
Skiing (cross-country)	42.0	10.0
Squash	52.5	12.5
Swimming (freestyle)	40.0	9.5
Table tennis	16.8	4.0
Tennis (social)	28.5	6.8
Typing	6.7	1.6
Volleyball	11.7	2.8
Walking briskly	29.5	7.0
upstairs	39.0	9.3
downstairs	13.0	3.1

Chart adapted from Recommended Nutrient Intakes, NHMRC Australia

Index

a

f

g

h

t

Z